T0224487

# Communications
# in Computer and Information Science　　1216

*Commenced Publication in 2007*
Founding and Former Series Editors:
Simone Diniz Junqueira Barbosa, Phoebe Chen, Alfredo Cuzzocrea,
Xiaoyong Du, Orhun Kara, Ting Liu, Krishna M. Sivalingam,
Dominik Ślęzak, Takashi Washio, Xiaokang Yang, and Junsong Yuan

## Editorial Board Members

Joaquim Filipe ⓘ
*Polytechnic Institute of Setúbal, Setúbal, Portugal*
Ashish Ghosh
*Indian Statistical Institute, Kolkata, India*
Igor Kotenko ⓘ
*St. Petersburg Institute for Informatics and Automation of the Russian
Academy of Sciences, St. Petersburg, Russia*
Raquel Oliveira Prates ⓘ
*Federal University of Minas Gerais (UFMG), Belo Horizonte, Brazil*
Lizhu Zhou
*Tsinghua University, Beijing, China*

More information about this series at http://www.springer.com/series/7899

Wenxing Hong · Chao Li ·
Qing Wang (Eds.)

# Technology-Inspired Smart Learning for Future Education

29th National Conference on Computer Science
Technology and Education, NCCSTE 2019
Kaifeng, China, October 9–11, 2019
Revised Selected Papers

Springer

*Editors*
Wenxing Hong 🆔
Xiamen University
Xiamen, China

Chao Li
Tsinghua University
Beijing, China

Qing Wang
Tianjin University
Tianjin, China

ISSN 1865-0929          ISSN 1865-0937   (electronic)
Communications in Computer and Information Science
ISBN 978-981-15-5389-9          ISBN 978-981-15-5390-5   (eBook)
https://doi.org/10.1007/978-981-15-5390-5

This Springer imprint is published by the registered company Springer Nature Singapore Pte Ltd.
The registered company address is: 152 Beach Road, #21-01/04 Gateway East, Singapore 189721, Singapore

# Preface

Smart learning environments are very diverse: massive open online courses with AI assistants, intelligent tutoring systems, interactive learning courseware, learning games, collaborative programming communities, community tutorial systems, personalized exercise programs, and tutoring robotics are all examples, especially in off-campus scenarios. A growing number of current campus-based courses in popular fields are also involved. All share a common purpose to increase human potential, leveraging data collection, data analysis, human interaction, and varying forms of computational assessment, adaptation, and guidance.

Information technologies have been proposed to the modern smart learning space, but may instead increase the digital divide if applied without reflection. So, further work is needed to understand how to leverage technologies to provide equitable education for all, and many questions still need to be answered. What are the main barriers to providing educational opportunities to underserved teachers and learners? How can AI and advanced technologies help overcome these difficulties? How can this work be done ethically? etc. The current proceedings gather the collective intelligence of the community to provide innovative and creative solutions, and thus try to investigate "Technology-Inspired Smart Learning".

March 2020

Wenxing Hong
Chao Li
Qing Wang

# Organization

## Program Chairs

| | |
|---|---|
| Wenxing Hong | Xiamen University, China |
| Chao Li | Tsinghua University, China |
| Qing Wang | Tianjin University, China |

## Program Committee

| | |
|---|---|
| Binyue Cui | Hebei University of Economics and Business, China |
| Wenxing Hong | Xiamen University, China |
| Jie Hu | Zhejiang University, China |
| Haoxiang Lang | University of Ontario Institute of Technology, Canada |
| Carsten Lecon | University of Applied Sciences Aalen, Germany |
| Chao Li | Tsinghua University, China |
| Taoshen Li | Guangxi University, China |
| Maoqing Li | Xiamen University, China |
| Xin Li | Louisiana State University, USA |
| Fengxia Li | Beijing Institute of Technology, China |
| Yan Qiang | Taiyuan University of Technology, China |
| Clarence W. de Silva | The University of British Columbia, Canada |
| Chunzhi Wang | Hubei University of Technology, China |
| Dan Wang | Chongqing University, China |
| Qing Wang | Tianjin University, China |
| Yang Weng | Sichuan University, China |
| Li Zheng | Tsinghua University, China |
| Wei Zhou | Beijing Jiaotong University, China |
| Shunzhi Zhu | Xiamen University of Technology, China |

# Contents

# Smart Learning

# Reform Method of Training Plan for Computer-Major Students Under 'Excellent Engineer Training Plan 2.0'

Juanjuan Zhao[✉], Yan Qiang, Mengnan Wang, Yunyun Dong, Xiaoling Ren, and Zhenqing Zhang

Graduate School of Information and Computer Science, Taiyuan University of Technology, Taiyuan 030600, China zhaojuanjuan@tyut.edu.cn

**Abstract.** The 'Plan for Educating and Training Excellent Engineers 2.0' implemented by the Ministry of Education (hereinafter referred to as excellent engineer training plan 2.0) is a milestone in the development of higher education in China. The new industrial revolution has raised new demands and challenges for university engineering education. According to the signal of large-scale development of excellent engineer training, this paper, from the training objectives of computer majors in the excellent engineer training plan 2.0, analyzes the key problems in the implementation of the training plan for students majoring in computer science in our university and discusses the reform method of the training plan, which brings forth new ideas in the excellent engineer training plan and explores a path of sustainable development.

**Keywords:** Excellent engineer training plan 2.0 · Computer majors · Teaching reform

## 1 Introduction

Since the achievements of 'excellent engineer training plan 1.0' are not completely consistent with the design concept and expected results, to adapt and lead the needs and challenges of the fourth industrial revolution, an upgraded version known as excellent engineer training plan 2.0 was proposed [1]. According to the Opinions on Accelerating the Development of New Engineering Projects and Implementing of Outstanding Engineer Education and Training Plan 2.0 issued by the Ministry of Education, the Ministry of Industry and Information Technology, and the Chinese Academy of Engineering on September 17, 2018, institutions of higher education, as the key players in the implementation of excellent engineer training plan 1.0, have some problems in promoting the plan. Therefore, to better implement the excellent engineer training plan 2.0, colleges and universities should focus on the reform and innovation of engineering talent training plan, explore an outstanding engineer training development path that combines their own characteristics with the advantages of excellent engineer training plan 2.0. The implementation of "Excellent training Plan 2.0" will provide strong intellectual support and talent support for the smooth implementation of national

© Springer Nature Singapore Pte Ltd. 2020
W. Hong et al. (Eds.): NCCSTE 2019, CCIS 1216, pp. 3–11, 2020.
https://doi.org/10.1007/978-981-15-5390-5_1

strategies such as "Innovation Drives Development", "Made in China 2025" and "the Belt and Road", it will lay a solid foundation for China to become a powerful country in world engineering education and to upgrade China's core competitiveness and comprehensive national strength.

With the continuous expansion of the number and scale of undergraduate colleges, the traditional training mode, the lagging teaching resources construction, and the single training environment have brought many problems that need urgent solutions to the cultivation of computer talents. As a representative engineering university of 211 Project in Shanxi Province, Taiyuan University of Technology is one of the first institutions implementing the excellent engineer training plan 1.0. Since its computer science and technology major was included as an experimental major of "excellent engineer training plan 1.0", this university has aimed to cultivate outstanding engineers to meet the needs of national, regional, and industrial economic construction and social development. Furthermore, from the perspective of reform of existing training programs, this university, by innovating practical teaching mode, creating research experimental environment, solving various engineering problems of the experimental project, and deepening school-enterprise cooperation, has found a way to train students to adapt to society quickly and cultivate excellent applied talents of engineering technology.

However, the existing training plan of the school of information and computer science for students majoring in computer science cannot meet the needs of excellent engineer training plan 2.0. Thus, we should make innovations in the existing training plan, and establish a teaching program specifically for the cultivation of outstanding computer talents. Our purpose is to further enhance students' innovative thinking ability, basic practical skills, engineering methods, hands-on ability, and development ability, so that students can have good self-learning ability at work and adapt to the rapid development of society, and are competent for computer related engineering jobs [2].

## 2    Current Situation of Practice of 'Excellent Engineer Training Plan'

The teaching mode of excellent engineer training plan 1.0 for computer major students is a '3 + 1' one which has 3 years of school teaching and 1 year of enterprise teaching. School-enterprise cooperation makes up for the shortcomings of our computer major students in conventional education and innovation ability training. The following problems have emerged in the implementation of this teaching mode:

(1) The entrepreneurship education of college students has not been paid enough attention to. The entrepreneurship education is still personalized for elites, which is not suitable for general public and leads to a lack of entrepreneurial ability of students. Lack of training and teaching of college students' entrepreneurial ability, neglecting the cultivation of college students' entrepreneurial practical skills. This educational concept leads to the lack of students' entrepreneurial ability. As a

result, after graduation, college students have weak self-employment concepts and lack of practical skills.

(2) A powerful nation relies on its education, and a good education requires excellent teachers. While implementing the excellent engineer training plan 2.0, many young engineering teachers have always been in a passive position in the development of scientific research. They lack understanding and grasp of scientific research methods and processes, and lack the ability to conduct independent research activities. As a consequence, they generally show a lack of innovation ability and engineering practice ability.

(3) On the one hand, Colleges and universities have insufficient understanding of the importance of school-enterprise cooperation. They cannot profoundly recognize that the characteristics of vocational education are to cultivate skilled talents that meet the needs of the market. As a result, colleges and universities have not paid enough attention to the work of school-enterprise cooperation. As a result, colleges and universities have not paid enough attention to the work of school-enterprise cooperation, lacking comprehensive and systematic planning and accurately positioning the level of cooperation. The system for carrying out school-enterprise cooperation is not perfect, and it is too much to consider its own immediate interests, affecting the implementation and development of specific work, and cannot improve the quality and efficiency of cooperation. On the other hand, enterprises do not have a strong desire to train students. The core technologies and major research and development projects of enterprises are confidential information, so the purpose of school-enterprise cooperation education cannot be truly realized. Furthermore, some students have different attitudes towards learning in enterprise from at school and they do not take this process as part of their undergraduate study.

(4) The traditional teaching evaluation system assesses students through their examination results, which fails to judge the students' real ability. In addition, the current evaluation standard is too simplified that it runs counter to the principle that the training of computer major students should focus on practice. A lot of examination contents require students' memory only. As a result, the students' enthusiasm in studying is not high and ability in practice is poor.

## 3   Targeted Reform and Innovation

To address the abovementioned problems existing in entrepreneurship education, teacher's ability, foreign cooperation mechanism, school-enterprise cooperation mode, and examination mode while implementing excellent engineer training plan 2.0, our school, namely, the school of information and computer science of Taiyuan University of Technology, plans to explore an educational system that is suitable for computer majors and in line with the training purpose of outstanding computer talents.

### 3.1  Changing the Concept of Entrepreneurship Education

In order to build a new entrepreneurship education system that activates students' innovation spirits and entrepreneurship, and to create conditions for the comprehensive development of students, our school, following the rules of outstanding engineers training, the law of education and teaching, and the law of national policy making, has re-examined the requirements, standards, and objectives of excellent engineer training plan 2.0. The training plan of entrepreneurship education for computer majors is as follows:

(1) **Creating a cultural environment for entrepreneurship.** Creating a good and appropriate learning environment for college students is the primary factor in fostering outstanding engineers in entrepreneurship education. The leaders of our college and school attach great importance to entrepreneurship education and propose to adopt appropriate performance assessing methods, and encourage teachers to set up more project teams of the same characteristics as TRoMac (an intelligent vehicle research and development team). Besides, our school makes full use of the campus media as well as traditional media and new media for publicity, and actively promotes the formation of entrepreneurship ideas among college students through innovation competition, entrepreneurship competition, entrepreneurship BBS, entrepreneurship form, and other brand activities. Publicize the government's new policy on college students' entrepreneurship, actively promote college students to form entrepreneurial concepts, cultivate students' willingness to innovate and dare to start a business, and form a campus innovation and entrepreneurship culture.

(2) **Building a platform for entrepreneurship education.** Increasing the content of entrepreneurship education, increasing the proportion of credit hours, and constructing a scientific and rational curriculum system and practice links that meet the learning needs of students are important guarantees for entrepreneurial education to train outstanding engineers. Our school has built a classroom teaching system integrating professional education and entrepreneurship education, and a curriculum system that combines basic courses, specialized courses, and practical courses of entrepreneurship. Besides, our school offers elective courses on innovation and entrepreneurship, entrepreneurship guidance, and entrepreneurship methods, as well as practical training on entrepreneurship development and quality development [3].

(3) **Building a new entrepreneurship service platform.** Providing policy support, conditional guarantees, and guiding services for students is a key part of entrepreneurship education to train outstanding engineers. The college cooperates with the enterprise to hire senior corporate executives with practical experience to serve as innovative and entrepreneurial instructors to ensure that students receive professional guidance from teachers at all stages of entrepreneurship. Our school will provide the students with one-stop service to start their own businesses, and offer open, equipment-support entrepreneurship labs as well as entrepreneurial studios free of rent or property management fees, so as to ensure their entrepreneurship projects are launched with "zero cost".

## 3.2  Building Better Teams of Young Engineering Teachers

"Excellent Plan 2.0" participates in colleges and universities to build a high-level teaching team with certain engineering experience. Full-time teachers must have experience in engineering practice and participate in the actual engineering projects or research and development projects of the company in a planned manner. Some of the teachers must have a certain number of years of enterprise work experience. Part-time teachers should be selected from the engineering and technical personnel and managers who have rich experience in engineering practice. In view of the characteristics of computer majors, the requirements on the practical ability and innovation ability of young engineering teachers are clearly put forward when recruiting young teachers. Especially those teachers who are responsible for teaching tasks such as practice teaching and curriculum design, the assessment of their engineering practice ability, innovation ability and other engineering abilities are emphasized in the recruitment. Young engineering teachers should face their own weaknesses and shortcomings and constantly improve their educational attainment and moral standards so as to open a new chapter in the computer education of our school. The construction plan of young engineering teachers of computer science is as follows:

(1) Our school should offer systematic engineering practice training courses for young teachers. Our school should not assign lots of scientific research tasks to young teachers right after they are employed. Instead, systematic engineering practice training courses and innovation ability training courses should be provided to help them gain more practical experiences and improve their innovation ability.

(2) Excellent engineer training plan 2.0, as an important part of the National Medium- and Long-term Plans for Educational Reform and Development, shows the strong support of the state for higher education. Therefore, the school should seize this opportunity and give more preferential policies to the young teachers who are willing to make bold innovations and think outside the box, and to undertake experimental courses and engineering practice teaching.

(3) In addition to the "going global strategy and bringing-in strategy", our school encourages young engineering teachers to practice and study in production enterprises and offer reasonable subsidies on the premise of not affecting teaching tasks. Moreover, our school should send young teachers to well-known foreign universities to learn teaching experience. Furthermore, our school should invite famous external technical experts and workers to give guidance on course design and practical teaching. Encourage teachers to participate in international conferences and enhance international influence. As more and more new teachers have overseas study and work experience, they can be encouraged to use existing resources to invite overseas partners to come to the colleges and universities for academic exchanges, promote international cooperation, and increase work enthusiasm [9].

(4) Our school should encourage young teachers to establish an innovative academic group, in which the teachers focus on research projects and cooperate with and encourage each other to maximize the scientific research output, so as to enrich the knowledge resources and improve the innovation ability of the group.

(5) The college encourages teaching and learning, teachers and students to grow together, guiding new teachers to attach importance to teaching, and acquiring the pedagogy and psychology knowledge required for teaching and educating people is a subtle process. Therefore, the college put forward the idea of letting new teachers grow together with students. Before they officially go to the podium, they can let teachers form a good teacher-student relationship with students [6].

### 3.3  Further Developing

At present, the school-enterprise cooperative education in our school is a supplement to the classroom teaching. The purpose is to know the true needs of enterprises by turning the classroom teaching to enterprise practice, so that the students can combine what they've learnt in class with the practical needs. Thus, our school plans to further deepen the school-enterprise collaborative training mode to promote the development of practical talents. The school-enterprise collaborative education plan for computer majors is as follows:

(1) The training subject of excellent engineer program is students, and thus focus should be put on the development of students. Therefore, it is quite important to choose the appropriate enterprise which is a platform for cultivating students' practical ability. In order to meet the purpose of improving students' practical operation ability and at the same time to ensure students' ideological education and personal safety outside, our school plans to have a deeper understanding of enterprises with cooperative intentions, and select enterprises that are representatives of the industry and have a high sense of responsibility. In this way, students can further enhance their practical ability and improve their professional ethics through the influence of excellent corporate culture [8].

(2) Not only the school and enterprise but also the students should participate in making the plan for school-enterprise collaborative training. In this process, our school should fully respect students' personal opinions, and actively promote the school-enterprise collaborative training program based on the comprehensive development of students. When studying in enterprises, students should give regular feedback on the learning progress so that our school and the enterprises can adjust the training process accordingly to hit the goal of school-enterprise collaborative education [4].

(3) Exploring practical plans for computer-based students, finding suitable corporate collaborative construction practice education bases, aiming to integrate education, training and research, not only to ensure the students' practical process, but also to achieve school-enterprise docking and to train engineering students who meet the needs of the company. At the same time, the development of technology can promote the adjustment of the student training plan, and then put forward new requirements for students to achieve the joint training of students and schools.

(4) As a leader in cultivating students, teachers also need to improve their engineering practice ability. Most of the company's tutors do not have lecture experience. How to improve the ability of schools and enterprise teachers is also the key to deepening the joint training of schools and enterprises. Strengthening the learning and communication between different teachers has become an important part of the training process.

## 3.4   Reforming Student Assessment Methods

In combination with the new requirements put forward by the excellent engineer training plan 2.0, our school, by learning new methods from the teaching system of other universities, changing the previous assessment mode, focusing on the cultivation of students' comprehensive ability, aims to establish a comprehensive and multi-level evaluation method of teaching results. The reform of assessment methods should be based on the improvement of teaching quality and comprehensively improve the core literacy of students. To change the concept of assessment, optimize the content and type of assessment, change the assessment form, and improve and perfect the assessment system, we must focus on the students and implement the focus of the education examination on cultivating and improving the core literacy of students. The reform plan of assessment method for students majoring in computer science is as follows:

(1) The current simple and unitary assessment method of curriculum is not conducive to encouraging students to participate in classroom teaching. To address this problem, our school proposes an automatic assessment mode for the whole training process, as shown in Fig. 1. By adding an assessment to each stage of the teaching process, including homework, quizzes, sectional examinations, on-line interaction, and offline interaction, evaluation on students' ability of memorizing basic theoretical knowledge is reduced, yet assessment on students' comprehensive ability of solving specific problems is increased. In the assessment, process evaluation is emphasized. Students' abilities are assessed based on their on-line time, homework accuracy, and amount of codes, so as to obtain the analytical report of students' comprehensive abilities. Then, according to the evaluation results, the teaching scheme is adjusted, and continuous process evaluation is conducted. By this way,

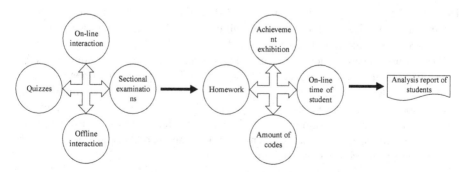

**Fig. 1.** The automatic assessment system for the whole training process

students are constantly motivated and their abilities to think divergently and put into practice what they have learned are improved, thereby giving full play to the role of assessment system in teaching process for diagnosis, motivation and guidance [5].

(2) The current knowledge memory-centered examination mode should be altered. In some of the exams of reformed subjects, students who take part in the exam will be given a piece of paper printed with some knowledge for reference during the exam. The purpose is to focus on students' application of knowledge instead of memorizing it. In addition, the test form is more flexible, which raises the requirements for both students and teachers [10].

(3) In the excellent engineer training program, it is a major task to improve students' engineering practice ability. Therefore, it is necessary to improve the proportion of students' engineering practice ability in the assessment. To this end, our school plans to include some representative computer competition results into the final assessment. Besides, our school plans to adopt the performance results of Teaching Practice and Engineering Ability Training of China Computer Federation so that the students can improve their own coding ability.

(4) Strengthen exchanges within the school, promote the model of examination reform, and form an assessment and reward mechanism. The assessment reform requires the strong support of the college, and it is more necessary for the teachers to actively participate in the assessment reform. Schools should formulate a series of related supporting incentive measures. For teaching and research rooms or teachers who carry out assessment reform research and achieve good reform effects, the school must give certain rewards to the teachers to actively participate in the assessment reform. The school can hold a symposium on teaching assessment reform on a regular basis. Through the speeches of teachers and students, we can timely understand and summarize the achievements and problems in the process of examination reform, and we should promote and learn from the experience of exam reforms with good results. The existed problem should be adjusted in time to improve teaching [7].

## 4   Conclusions

This paper discusses the problems, which will affect the training of computer engineers, in the entrepreneurial ideas, engineering ability of young teachers, simple evaluation mode, and school-enterprise cooperation mode of the current training plan for computer major students under excellent engineer training plan. Guided by the training objective of excellent engineer training plan 2.0, reform methods are proposed corresponding to the above problems. At the same time, our school attempts to develop a training system suitable for computer talents. In this way, our school can provide other colleges or universities with some scientific and useful suggestions for reference, so as to give full play to the advantages of excellent engineer training plan 2.0 and cultivate more outstanding engineering talents for China.

# References

1. Zhu, Z., Li, M.: Reflections on the implementation of excellent engineer education training plan 2.0. High. Eng. Educ. Res. **1**, 46–53 (2018)
2. Guo, X., Shi, L., Song, X.: On the cultivation of application - oriented undergraduate talents under the environment of "excellent engineer program" – a case study of computer science. E-Commer. **9**, 80–81 (2014)
3. Xue, H., Xue, Z.: Integration of innovation and entrepreneurship education and excellent engineer training. Educ. Career **6** (2016)
4. Li, L.: Thinking and practice on the integration of school-enterprise culture under the background of "excellent engineer training program"–a case study of automation major of Beijing institute of petrochemical technology. Educ. Teach. BBS **46** (2017)
5. Jin, W.: Reform of examination methods from the perspective of core literacy. Teach. Manag. (Theory Ed.) **10** (2017)
6. Chen, S., Huang, P.: Training and support of newly introduced young teachers in engineering colleges under new engineering background. High. Educ. J. (2018)
7. Guo, G.: On the development and transformation of self-taught examination and the reform of examination content and form. Adult Educ. **36**(4) (2016)
8. Feng, Y.: The practical dilemma and guarantee mechanism of school-enterprise cooperation and double-main body running schools in higher vocational colleges. Heilongjiang High. Educ. Res. **6**, 84–87 (2019)
9. Zhuang, Y., et al.: Adhere to the problem-oriented approach and improve the quality of young teachers in universities and colleges in the new era. Chin. High. Educ. **623**(05), 34–36 (2019)
10. Zhou, C., Li, Y.-H.: The reform of Japanese university entrance examination: goals, paths and challenges. Comp. Educ. Res. **5** (2019)

# Construction of Practical Teaching System for Integration of Specialism and Innovation Based on Virtual Simulation Technology

Yangping Wang[1,2(✉)], Jianwu Dang[1,2,3], Jiu Yong[2,3],
Wenrun Wang[2,3], and Biao Yue[2,3]

[1] School of Electronic and Information Engineering,
Lanzhou Jiaotong University, Lanzhou, China
w_yp73@163.com
[2] National Computer Science and Technology Experimental Teaching
Demonstration Center, Lanzhou Jiaotong University, Lanzhou, China
[3] Gansu Provincial Engineering Research Center for Artificial Intelligence
and Graphics and Image Processing, Lanzhou, China

**Abstract.** The practical teaching for the majors of rail transit in colleges and universities involves a large number of high-cost, high-consumption, large-scale or comprehensive training. It will often encounter high-risk or extreme environment, inaccessible or irreversible operation, which seriously affects the cultivation of students professional engineering ability. In this paper, a practical teaching system based on virtual simulation technology is constructed for rail transit specialty. The system integrates the professional advantages and practical platform in the university, develops virtual simulation experimental teaching resources and practical teaching cases, and enables students to carry out "independent, cooperative and inquiry" learning in an open, safe, realistic and interactive virtual environment. This system will enhance students professional engineering practice ability and innovation ability, promote the training level of rail transit professionals and the overall quality of students. And for students, it can achieve the goal of strengthening the basic principles of curriculum, training design and research thinking, and enhancing innovation and entrepreneurship ability.

**Keywords:** Virtual simulation · Integration of specialism and innovation · Practical teaching system · Teaching cases

## 1 Introduction

Virtual reality (VR) technology and equipment have achieved rapid development and application in various industries. In the field of education, VR will reform student's learning style after multimedia and computer teaching, and realize the learning of "anytime, anywhere, anybody and any content". It can fully mobilize the interest of learners, and makes them enter any realistic learning environment and immerse in learning. Thus extremely improve the effectiveness of learning. Creating a realistic virtual practice teaching environment through virtual simulation technology will not only play an epoch-making role in promoting the reform of the whole field of education, but also achieve cross-regional and cross-border sharing of educational resources, promote the balance of educational resources, and enhance the level of education of citizens. In recent years, virtual simulation technology has been listed as the focus of education informationization. The Ministry of Education of China clearly requests colleges and universities throughout the country to vigorously promote the deep integration and wide application of virtual simulation technology and higher education. It is necessary to deepen the reform of innovation and entrepreneurship education in colleges and universities, and promote the close integration of innovation and entrepreneurship education with professional education.

In recent years, Chinese rail transit construction, represented by high-speed railways, has made remarkable achievement. In the vigorous development of the "going out" strategy, it has increasingly become an important engine of "one belt and one road" initiative. The major specialties of rail transit involve the operation management, locomotive control, communication signal, traction power supply and so on. The operation process of rail transit has the characteristics of huge complexity, multi-link, strong coupling, high risk and irreversibility. In the process of practical teaching, there are high speed, high density, and train control endangers traffic safety. The fault scenarios can't be reproduced, the scale is huge, the scene can only be seen and can't be practiced, and the real environment can't reproduce the difficulties of wireless channel, network planning, high-speed rail wireless communication handover in the complex terrain. In the experiment and training, it involves high-risk or extreme environment, unreachable or irreversible operation, and expensive. It is difficult to carry out on-the-spot practical teaching for students, in the case of time consuming, large-scale or comprehensive training. Because the virtual practice environment is not limited by physical space, the construction cost of multi-professional practice platform is greatly reduced, and the learning model required for the practice environment can be quickly iterated [1–3]. Based on virtual simulation technology, we can construct a realistic experimental teaching environment, which provide an innovative and integrated practical teaching system that integrates interdisciplinary, interdisciplinary, intertechnical, professional learning and innovative design. It is conducive to reducing costs, breaking time and space boundaries, and improving the innovative and entrepreneurial practice and the cultivation of students innovative and practical ability in professional practice [4]. Therefore, using virtual simulation technology, transforming innovation and creation in engineering practice into new products of educational technology in time, and building a highly simulation and rich virtual simulation experiment system [5, 6] has become an inevitable requirement for rail transit personnel training.

In this paper, an innovative comprehensive practical teaching system based on virtual simulation technology and the combination of virtual and reality is constructed based on the practical teaching requirements of rail transit specialty in Lanzhou Jiaotong University. It uses the characteristics of virtual simulation technology such as great immersion, strong interaction and inexpensive [7, 8] to solve the problem, which can't be done in the integrated education of innovative entrepreneurship and professional courses. To solve the problems of not doing well, we should form a practical teaching system of deep integration of the professional courses of foundation design innovation and innovative education. It can improve students professional quality and comprehensive innovation ability, and promote the overall improvement of the level of personnel training and the overall quality of students in colleges and universities.

## 2    Combining the Virtual with the Real to Construct a Practical Teaching System of Integration of Creativity and Practice

Make full use of the existing professional education and innovative entrepreneurship education practice teaching platform [9, 10], and build an innovative integration practice teaching system based on virtual simulation technology, which combines virtual and real, to solve the problems of difficult practice teaching and insufficient degree of integration of innovative and related specialties in schools. Lanzhou Jiaotong University is a rail transit university with distinctive characteristics. Many national experimental teaching platforms are built in this university to provide experimental teaching services for students, such as "Traffic Information Innovative Talents Training Model Experimental Zone", "Virtual Simulation Experimental Teaching Center for Rail Transit Information and Control", "Experimental Teaching Demonstration Center for Comprehensive Innovation of Information and Control", and "Computer Experiment Teaching Demonstration Center". Integration innovation training on students is conducted by relevant departments and professional teams such as "College of Innovation and Entrepreneurship", "Artificial Intelligence Specialized Maker Space in Gansu Province", "Teaching Team of Information and Control Innovation and Entrepreneurship Education of Rail Transit" in Gansu Province, and a number of innovation and entrepreneurship base teaching teams. Based on hardware and software resources in the university, this paper integrates virtual simulation technology into the practice teaching of students innovation and entrepreneurship, organizes and trains students to participate in professional disciplines competitions, stimulates students interest in learning, cultivates students scientific research literacy, strengthens the cultivation of students thinking innovation ability and independent creativity ability. The method focuses on the cultivation of teachers and students qualities, breaking the barriers of innovative and integrated education, taking students as the center, building an interdisciplinary, interdisciplinary and inter-technical virtual simulation and innovative and integrated practical teaching system, making representative cases of virtual simulation and innovative and integrated practical teaching, and promoting virtual imitation. The concrete structure of the application of real technology in the practice teaching of creative integration is shown in Fig. 1.

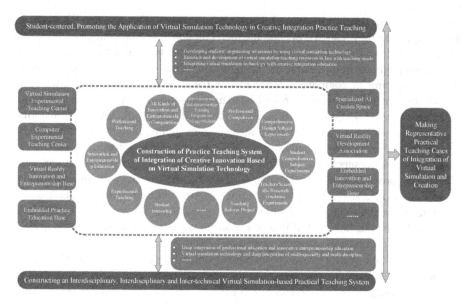

**Fig. 1.** The practical teaching system of integration of creativity based on virtual simulation technology

For example, the project "Virtual Interactive Learning System of Railway Signal Equipment Based on Hardware Perception Device", which guides students to complete the training plan for college students innovation and entrepreneurship, is difficult for students and practitioners of rail transit majors to grasp. In traditional teaching, powerpoint, graphics and text are used to explain it usually. However, in the process of on-the-spot teaching, there are some difficulties, such as train speed, high density, train control endangering traffic safety, large scale, on-site can only be seen and can't be operated, and the real environment can't be reproduced the real railway signal equipment, which makes it difficult to understand the internal structure of the railway signal equipment. Through the research and development of 3D interactive experimental system of virtual rail transit signal equipment based on hardware perception, the 3D virtual signal equipment can be controlled by hardware perception equipment, and the internal components, compositions and operating environment of the equipment can be known at any time, so that students can quickly understand the functions of the railway signal equipment and the signal equipment in the railway station yard. Actual action principle is helpful for students to master the knowledge points of railway traffic signal equipment, computer and art design. The implementation of this project relies on the VR base, the software and hardware resources of the virtual simulation experimental teaching center, and the VR developer association. "Virtual Railway Signal Equipment Interactive Learning System Based on Hardware Perception Device" combines the students of rail transit, computer and art design specialties, and simulates the course knowledge points which are difficult to grasp in the practical teaching of the specialty by virtual means, as well as some knowledge points of the specialty courses which are difficult to carry out practical teaching. Students major in rail transit control railway signaling equipment through hardware equipment. Through the 3D model of the equipment, they can know the internal components and composition of the equipment at any time. It is easier to understand the internal structure of railway signaling equipment in the course of "Introduction to Railway". By making the work, students majoring in computer science master the knowledge points of serial communication, analog-to-digital conversion, data transmission, etc. in the course of "Microcomputer Interface and Principle". Through this work, students majoring in art and design learn in-depth three-dimensional modeling, unity scene building and other knowledge points. Finally, they can integrate their works into innovative entrepreneurship competitions for college students, accumulate experience and continuously improve their works. In order to pave the way for the subsequent business incubation, and teachers and students can organize their works for virtual simulation to integrate practical teaching resources and write experimental guides, which can provide guidance for the development of innovative business practice and open experiments in the follow-up professional courses.

Relying on the platform and professional team of the University, this study integrates virtual simulation technology into the innovation and entrepreneurship practice teaching of college students, organizes and trains students to participate in professional subject competitions, stimulates students' interest in learning, cultivates students' scientific research literacy, and strengthens the cultivation of students' thinking innovation ability and independent innovation ability. For example, the project of "interactive learning system of virtual railway signal equipment based on hardware sensing equipment" has won the first prize in the 15th "Bochuang Cup" national embedded artificial intelligence design competition for college students. It has not only integrated the professional teaching depth into innovation and entrepreneurship, but also greatly stimulated students learning enthusiasm. In addition, through participating in the training of innovation and entrepreneurship, academic exchanges and cooperation and professional training organized inside and outside the school, teachers and students have gradually become the backbone of both virtue and talent with solid theoretical basis, rich practical experience and advanced technical level, and have created and integrated practical teaching specially for virtual simulation of various disciplines and specialties in the school. Learning lays a solid foundation.

## 2.1 Push Forward the Application of Virtual Simulation Technology in the Practice Teaching of Creative Integration with Students as the Center

Through the implementation of the experimental teaching mode of "student-centered, learning oriented, problem-oriented, task driven", starting from the needs of "special creative integration" personnel training in the construction and selection of virtual simulation resources, this method is student-oriented, which can mobilize students' enthusiasm and initiative in learning, enhance students' awareness of innovation and creation, and pay attention to knowledge transfer, ability training and quality enhanced collaborative implementation. It integrates virtual simulation resources and physical simulation experiment courses organically [6], emphasizes the combination of virtual and real, and promotes the application of virtual simulation technology in the teaching plan, teaching arrangement, experimental equipment and site, experimental teaching teachers, etc. in the practice teaching of professional innovation integration. In view of the fact that the existing virtual simulation experimental teaching resources are difficult to meet the needs of specialized experimental teaching in schools, and the professional knowledge and teaching experience of enterprise technicians in virtual simulation resources development on the market are not systematic, the compatibility between the developed experimental resources and the teaching syllabus is not high, and the development cost of virtual simulation experimental teaching resources is relatively high. By summing up and integrating the existing virtual simulation experimental teaching resources, teachers can guide students to develop virtual simulation experimental teaching resources according to the development of teaching syllabus and new professional technologies, develop virtual simulation experimental teaching resources for professional courses sustainably, and provide students with high-quality and complete experimental teaching of professional courses. Resources can also effectively improve students ability of engineering application and innovation and entrepreneurship. For example, "Virtual Interactive Learning System of Railway Signal Equipment Based on Hardware Perception Device" not only enables students to quickly understand the functions of railway signal equipment, but also controls the 3D model by hardware Perception Device to know the internal components and components of the equipment at any time, which helps students to master the knowledge points of the course.

## 2.2   Building an Interdisciplinary, Interdisciplinary and Inter-technical Virtual Simulation-Based Practical Teaching System

To discover the pain and difficulty in innovation and entrepreneurship education in disciplines and specialties, and make use of the advantages of virtual simulation and related technology, to build a reality that meets the teaching needs, takes into account both teaching and practice, has clear goals and contents, adapts to market demand, pays attention to enhancing user experience, and integrates virtual simulation and innovation practice teaching system. Supported by school innovation and entrepreneurship base, collaborative education base, student associations, undergraduate innovation and entrepreneurship training project, open experiment, education reform project and undergraduate innovation and entrepreneurship contest, virtual simulation technology is applied to innovative and entrepreneurship practice teaching of professional courses to build interdisciplinary, interdisciplinary and interdisciplinary. The virtual simulation innovation and practice teaching system with deep technology integration can improve students innovative spirit, entrepreneurial consciousness and innovative entrepreneurial ability in the professional field. For example, the innovation and entrepreneurship training plan project for college students, "virtual railway signal equipment interactive learning system based on hardware sensing equipment", builds a bridge between virtual simulation technology, multi-disciplinary and professional curriculum innovation and entrepreneurship education by forming teams of students majoring in art, electronics and computer and relying on the existing software and hardware experimental teaching resources of the school.

### 2.3    Making Representative Practical Teaching Cases of Integration of Virtual Simulation and Creation

According to the virtual simulation teaching system, relying on the existing VR real-time interactive VR helmet, VR data glove, 3D scanner, VR interactive curved surface screen and other advanced virtual simulation software and hardware interactive equipment, students are guided to complete a professional course practice teaching case and improve it. Optimize shortcomings of the case, summarize the problems encountered in the research and development, form a complete experimental guide, and apply the case to the later professional curriculum practice teaching, improve students practical innovation ability. For example, "Virtual Railway Signal Equipment Interactive Learning System Based on Hardware Perception Device" can be used as a case of virtual simulation experiment teaching. It can be applied to the practical teaching of a certain specialized course of rail transit, computer and art design. It can also guide the experiment and production practice by open experiment, student project innovation. Interested teachers and students can continuously improve and innovate the work to meet the requirements of college students' entrepreneurship incubation project.

## 3    Implementation of Integrative Practice Teaching Based on Virtual Simulation Technology

Virtual simulation experiment teaching vividly simulates the things and environment in the real world, and divides professional course knowledge into three kinds of experimental teaching contents: basic, design and innovation. It is conducive to the cultivation of students innovative practical ability in the process of professional experiment, and it also simulates the flow of production, management and social service in enterprises. Cheng helps students improve their entrepreneurial ability. Relying on the platform of innovation and entrepreneurship base, collaborative education base, software and hardware resources of virtual simulation experiment teaching center and student associations established by the school, the project of innovation and entrepreneurship training plan, open experiment, education reform project and innovation and entrepreneurship contest for college students are supported, and the students innovative spirit, entrepreneurship consciousness and entrepreneurship contest are supported. Focusing on the cultivation of innovation and entrepreneurship ability and taking the cultivation of students professional quality as the core, we should break the barrier of integration of virtual simulation technology and innovation education. The implementation process of creative integration practice teaching based on virtual simulation technology is shown in Fig. 2.

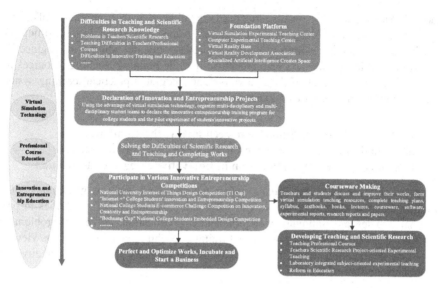

**Fig. 2.** Construction process of creative integration practice teaching system based on virtual simulation technology

By investigating the structure, content and form of virtual simulation technology in the innovation and entrepreneurship education of professional courses in colleges and universities, focusing on the improvement of students professional quality and the cultivation of their innovative and entrepreneurship ability, this paper summarizes and integrates the existing virtual simulation experimental teaching resources, according to the experimental teaching syllabus of professional courses and the development of new professional technologies. Guiding students to develop virtual simulation experimental teaching resources, and improving the ability of students innovation and entrepreneurship through innovative entrepreneurship training programs, open experiments, and competitions and training related to innovative entrepreneurship of College students. At the same time, several representative virtual simulation and creative integration practice teaching cases are produced and applied. In the follow-up practice teaching.

## 4    The Characteristics of the Practical Teaching System of Integration of Creativity and Innovation Based on Virtual Simulation Technology

By promoting the application of virtual simulation technology in creative integration practice teaching, we can build an interdisciplinary, interdisciplinary and inter-technical virtual simulation integration practice teaching system. Making a representative case of virtual simulation creative integration practice teaching, providing a case template for the follow-up development of virtual simulation creative integration teaching. To promote the application of virtual simulation technology in innovative and integrated practical teaching centered on students, teachers guide students from many colleges to organize a multi-disciplinary cross-integration team to develop virtual simulation experimental teaching resources, which improves students ability of engineering application and innovation and entrepreneurship while building teaching resources for schools. The main features of the innovative and integrated practical teaching system based on virtual simulation technology are as follows:

### 4.1 By Virtue of Virtual Simulation Technology, the Combination of Virtual and Real Can Solve the Problem that it is Difficult to Construct a Practical Platform in Innovative Integrated Education

Using the characteristics of virtual simulation technology, such as good immersion, strong interaction and low cost, we can solve the pain points and difficulties in professional courses and innovative entrepreneurship education, solve the problem of "can't do, can't do well," in experimental training teaching, cultivate students view of large-scale engineering, improve the ability of the students professional quality and comprehensive innovation.

### 4.2 Student-Centered, Virtual Simulation Technology-Based Construction of "Innovative Integration of Practical Teaching and Innovative Integration of Practical Teaching" Practice Teaching Resources Construction Model

Focusing on the cultivation of students innovative spirit, entrepreneurial consciousness and innovative entrepreneurial ability, focusing on the cultivation of students professional quality, focusing on the requirements of experimental teaching syllabus of professional courses and the latest development of industrial technology, the construction model of practical teaching resources for the integration of teachers and students mutually beneficial and mutually reinforcing innovations is constructed. At the same time, the construction of virtual simulation resources can improve students ability of engineering application and innovation and entrepreneurship.

## 5  Conclusion

Based on the existing practice teaching platform of the school and the combination of virtual and real, we construct a practical teaching system of integration of innovation and innovation based on virtual simulation technology, build a complete practice teaching platform for students professional curriculum education and innovation and entrepreneurship education, and integrate innovation and entrepreneurship education into professional education in an all-round way. To enable students to carry out autonomous learning in an open and interactive virtual environment, enhance the ability of the students engineering practice, innovation and entrepreneurship. Based on the developed virtual simulation resource development system and template, the virtual simulation experimental teaching resources jointly developed by teachers and students can provide support for the school's sustainable construction of virtual simulation and integration of practical teaching resources. The system of virtual simulation and the case of virtual simulation and integration of practical teaching can provide reference for teachers and students of all disciplines who carry out creative integration of practical teaching by means of virtual simulation experiment. At the same time, with the help of the existing internet experimental platform of the school, it is open to colleges, universities, at home and abroad, and can be used for brothers. Schools and related enterprises provide teaching and training services.

**Acknowledgment.** This research was financially supported by Gansu Science and Technology Project (Grant No. 18JR3RA104), Innovation and Entrepreneurship Course Construction Project of Lanzhou Jiaotong University in 2019 (2019CXCYKC10), Experimental Teaching Reform Research Project of Lanzhou Jiaotong University (2019007, 2019026).

# References

1. Lu, Y., Zhai, Z., Ma, J., et al.: Distributed virtual laboratory construction technology. Comput. Simul. (z1), 12–14 (2005)
2. Zhang, K., Zheng, B., Ciu, J., et al.: Exploration on the construction of virtual simulation experiment center of environmental engineering based on OBE model. Exp. Technol. Manage. **36**(01), 270–273 (2019)
3. Cui, G., Xiong, J.: Development of MOOE practical teaching platform based on virtual simulation technology. Exp. Technol. Manage. **33**(4), 103–107 (2016)
4. Long, Y., Li, Z., Li, Z.: Research on the deep integration of virtual simulation technology and innovation entrepreneurship education. Exp. Technol. Manage. (04), 118–120 (2018)
5. Li, H., Xia, H., Song, S.: Research and practice on innovative ability training mode of electronic information professionals based on new subjects. Exp. Technol. Manage. **36**(4), 200–202 (2019)
6. Cai, V., Chen, A., Wang, M., et al.: Construction of network experimental teaching system of virtual simulation experimental teaching center. Lab. Sci. (1), 121–123 (2018)
7. Hu, S., Zhang, C., Liu, H.: Exploration and practice of electrical logging experiment teaching based on virtual simulation technology. Petrol. Educ. (1), 74–77 (2017)
8. Chen, Y., Chen, S., Yang, L., et al.: Research and practice of PLC experimental teaching based on virtual simulation technology. Mach. Manuf. Autom. (2), 89–92 (2018)
9. Hu, C.: Reform and practice of constructing undergraduate practical training teaching system based on virtual simulation technology. Educ. Teach. Forum (14), 131–132 (2018)
10. Du, Y.: Research on the construction of experimental teaching center based on virtual simulation technology. Educ. Teach. Forum (15), 273–274 (2018)

# A Survey of Artificial Intelligence Techniques on MOOC of Legal Education

Yang Weng[1], Xuejiao Liang[1], Hanyan Duan[1], Songyuan Gu[2], Ning Wang[3], and Zhu Wang[2(✉)]

[1] College of Mathematics, Sichuan University, Chengdu, China
[2] Law School, Sichuan University, Chengdu, China
`wangzhu@scu.edu.cn`
[3] College of Information and Smart Electromechanical Engineering, Xiamen Huaxia University, Xiamen, China

**Abstract.** Legal education as well as the development of artificial intelligence has been introduced in this paper, and focuses on the application of artificial intelligence technology in legal education. In the process of making and updating the legal MOOC, it needs to be closely integrated with artificial intelligence technology. Such as making bilingual subtitles through machine translation, use the question and answer system to help intelligent teaching assistants, perform anti-cheat warning through face recognition, and update the curtain class through speech recognition and changing the mouth shape technology according to the text. Finally, we propose the direction in which artificial intelligence can develop in legal MOOC education.

**Keywords:** Artificial intelligence · Legal education · MOOC

## 1 Introduction

MOOC, short for Massive Open Online Courses, which is jointly proposed by Canadian scholar Dave Cormier and American scholar Bryan Alexander in 2008 [1]. It originally refers to the Connectivism and Connected Knowledge course (CCK08), an online course offered formally through the University of Manitoba, which was facilitated in 2008 by George Siemens and Stephen Downs from the University of Manitoba [2].

In 2012, three of the most influential MOOC platform companies in the world, Coursera, edX, Udacity, were born in the United States, known as the "Year of the MOOC" by The New York Times. By September 2019, the Coursera platform has offered 3818 courses, edX 2847 courses and Udacity 175 courses. In 2013, Peking University, Tsinghua University signed contracts with edX, Fudan University, Shanghai Jiaotong University signed with Coursera. At the

This work is partly supported by National Key R&D Program of China (Grant No. 2018YFC0830300).

© Springer Nature Singapore Pte Ltd. 2020
W. Hong et al. (Eds.): NCCSTE 2019, CCIS 1216, pp. 22–37, 2020.
https://doi.org/10.1007/978-981-15-5390-5_3

same time, the Wisdom Tree Online Education, the Chinese University MOOC and other domestic MOOC platforms developed, and its influence gradually expanded. Therefore, in 2013, called China's "MOOC Year" by the media. By September 2019, Wisdom Tree Online Education and Chinese University MOOC have offered more than 4000 courses respectively.

In recent years, legal education is facing three developments. First, law school of foreign universities is facing an economic crisis caused by low application rates, and some universities even begin to lay off staff [3]. Second, the gradual establishment of legal courses, for example, in 2013, Yale University Professor Akhil Amar introduced the Constitution course at Coursera, Harvard University Professor William Fisher offered a course in Copyright Law on edX, and Professor Lu Sixuan of Tianjin University opened The Clinical Legal Education Program on the Smart Tree Online Education Platform and Professor Jiang Guohua from Wuhan University have opened an administrative law course on the Chinese University MOOC. Third, some schools grant credits for law courses or course-based degrees, such as the University of Washington Law School, which provides American Law L.L.M degree courses for foreign students [3]. The latter two developments are closely related to MOOC, and the first development can be eliminated through the development of MOOC. Therefore, the MOOC promotes the development of legal education; but we should also see that the law curriculum has its own unique academic characteristics, such as subjective, logical and speculative content, and some of the learning content is of strong practicality, which makes the development of the MOOC face many challenges in the course of course opening, operation, renewal and maintenance.

The concept of artificial intelligence was first proposed by Turing [4]. "Turing test" is used to test whether machines can show intelligence equivalent to or indistinguishable from human beings. Recently, computer computing power has been greatly improved. Machine learning and deep learning have extremely high requirements on computing power. The computing power of cloud computing of 10 trillion times per second has promoted the development of artificial intelligence. The exponential growth of data solves the problem that algorithm training requires a large amount of data, which lays a foundation for the development of artificial intelligence. As the soul of artificial intelligence, many leading companies' open source or cloud services enable advanced technologies to spread rapidly, algorithms are packaged into easy-to-use products, and artificial intelligence has developed qualitatively.

Natural language processing is a very important part. Through natural language understanding and natural language generation, machine translation intelligent question and answer subtitles can be automatically generated online intelligent customer service, which will greatly improve people's work efficiency. Computer vision can identify objects and scenes by converting image signals. Computer vision plays a very important role in security, disease diagnosis and treatment, identification of suspects. Intelligent robots that integrate autonomous learning, reasoning, decision-making and other skills can replace human beings to complete some difficult tasks in harsh environments. Such as underwater operation, high-temperature operation and high-altitude operation.

More and more interdisciplinary subjects appear due to the excellent performance of artificial intelligence in various fields. However, the basic research of artificial intelligence is not closely related to application practice. Research and development technology is growing rapidly, but companies can't bring these advanced technologies to the ground, and they can't combine these technologies with practical applications. The combination of artificial intelligence and specific fields and the realization of research and development technology are urgent problems to be solved in the artificial intelligence industry.

In the production process of MOOC, manual production of subtitles requires multiple listening to audio, mastering legal professional knowledge and translation skills, which is a lot of work that consumes time and energy. Generating bilingual subtitles through speech recognition and machine translation can reduce the burden of work. Only check is required, the difference between the two workloads is self-evident.

In the learning process of MOOC, students can ask questions in the bulletin board in real time because they cannot understand the course content, and the intelligent assistant will give accurate answers in time. Students interact in real time during the learning process, which is conducive to the improvement of learning efficiency. Other students will also answer questions on their own initiative. We can see students' different understandings of the same problem, which will help the lecturer to explain a variety of different ideas in the next lecture.

In the process of MOOC examination, students with poor self-control cannot guarantee to watch the whole video carefully because there is no supervision, which is not conducive to students' increasing interest in learning, and is not conducive to ensuring the learning effect. A variety of artificial intelligence techniques can be used for anti-cheating warnings.

In the process of MOOC updating, some of the laws are updated very quickly, but only a few of them are updated according to the actual situation. At this time, the recorded videos will not be used in real time. Occasionally, there will be omissions and slippages. Re-shooting the video will take a lot of time and effort, but without modification, it will affect the viewing experience, so we can use artificial intelligence technology to make automatic updates, or lower cost updates.

In the production and operation of legal MOOCs, it is necessary to combine them closely with artificial intelligence technology, such as implementing bilingual subtitles through machine translation, intelligent assistant through intelligent question answering, anti-cheating warning by constructing student portraits, and the correspondence between the subtitle and the mouth is realized according to the speech recognition technology.

## 2   Legal Artificial Intelligence Translation

Machine Translation is a process of converting one natural language into another through computer programs, also known as automatic translation technology [5].

In 1954, Georgetown University in the United States successfully translated about 60 sentences of Russian into English automatically, which was regarded as the beginning of machine translation. In a report submitted in 1966 by the Automatic Language Processing Advisory Committee, the progress of machine translation research in the past decade was slow and did not exceeding the expectation. This stage of machine translation is mainly based on dictionary and grammar to generate translation, this rule-based machine translation (RBMT) has been very slow in the next two decades. Until the 1980s, with the development of computer computing power and the reduction of computing cost, statistical machine translation (SMT) developed rapidly. Statistical machine translation generates translation results based on analysis of bilingual text corpora.

In 1997, Ramoneco and Mikel Forcada proposed to use encoder-decoder structure for machine translation [6]. In 2003, a group of researchers led by Yoshua Bengio at the University of Montreal developed a language model based on neural networks [7]. In 2013, Nal Kalchbrenner and Phil Blunsom proposed a new end-to-end encoder-decoder architecture for machine translation [8]. It can be considered that this research result is the birth of neural machine translation (NMT). Neural machine translation is a method to obtain the mapping relation between natural languages by using deep learning neural network.

In 2014, Sutskever and Cho et al. developed a learning method called seq2seq, which can use RNN for both encoders and decoders [9,10]. In 2014, Yoshua Bengio's team introduced an attention mechanism to NMT [11], and neural machine translation developed rapidly. As shown in Fig. 1, we have given the intuitive model of seq2seq.

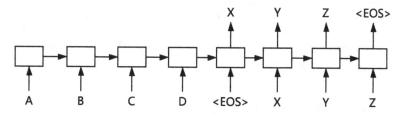

**Fig. 1.** The intuitive representation of the seq2seq model. Where A, B, C, and D represent inputs, <EOS> represents the terminator, X, Y, and Z represent outputs, and X also serves as the input to Y.

Since the terminology in the field of law differs greatly from the language in the general field, the machine translation technology required in the field differs from the machine translation technology in the field of general knowledge.

At the end of 1997, Babel Fish was launched as a translation program and was widely used by law researchers in the late 1990s. Yates [12] evaluated the accuracy of the Babel Fish translation program in translating legal texts. The conclusion is that Babel Fish is not suitable for use in the legal library. Kit [13] and others also compared the effects of various representative online machine translation systems in translating legal texts.

As Pedro Domingos said: "Do not against artificial intelligence, let artificial intelligence work for you". Unlike ordinary machine translation, machine translation for subtitle production of 1 legal MOOC requires special needs.

In 2018, the Microsoft team published Achieving Human Parity on Automatic Chinese to English News Translation. Through good engineering and algorithmic techniques, it is proved that the neural translation model can reach the level of translation comparable to humans in a specific field.

On April 12, 2019, the "Meta Cup" legal translation man-machine match competition jointly organized by Peking University Law Artificial Intelligence Laboratory and Shanghai Secret Tower Network Technology Co-hosting was held at Peking University Law School. The result of the competition was: the "Entity Team" consisting of a student and the "Meta MT" defeated the "elite team" composed of the top three in the human trials. In both speed and accuracy, AI has won.

There are very big differences between Chinese and English. The names of entities in legal statements are often too long. They may contain two or more entities. It is very difficult to identify entities during translation. Preliminary experiments show that the "Meta MT" can perform a better corresponding translation of the Chinese subtitles that have been broken. But before breaking the sentence, it is still very difficult to completely translate a long sentence. This can be a target direction of the next research by the relevant direction scholars.

The vocabulary of the legal profession has a fixed translation result, and the order in which the machine translation is automatically generated is often contrary to the legal terminology. Machine translation can't take into account the customary habits of people, and the accuracy of translation for fixed proverbs is very low. Some fixed words in law also need to be added to a specific user dictionary. How to automatically generate and update the user dictionary is also an urgent problem to be solved.

## 3   Intelligent Assistant

The concept of Question Answering was first proposed in the 1960s. The initial question-and-answer system was searched by a knowledge data set written by experts in a specific field. In 1961, Green designed BASEBALL [14], which can answer questions about the US professional baseball league season. With the development of artificial intelligence technology, a question answering system for different fields has emerged. Start [15] is the first web-based question answering system developed by the Massachusetts Institute of Technology in 1993. Start is a hybrid question answering system that takes advantage of the related technologies of KBQA [16,17]and WQA [18]. Start first attempts to answer the user's question through the knowledge base. Only when the knowledge base does not contain the answer required by the user, it will use the search engine to find relevant information and extract knowledge from it and return it to the user.

In 2005, P. Quaresma [19] provided a question answering system for the processing of relevant judicial documents for the Portuguese judiciary. Mi-Young Kim [20] proposed a legal question answering system using deep convolutional neural networks. It shows that the deep learning-based method is superior to the SVM based supervised model. At the same time, he also made related work and proposed a combination of rule-based and unsupervised models, which is superior to SVM-based supervision model [21].

In 2009, A Peñas [22] presented the first round of public question answer (QA) assessment tasks for European legislation at the 2009 Cross-Language Assessment Forum (CLEF). In 2010, he introduced the assessment task of the second round of public question answering for European legislation at the 2010 CLEF.

Question answering system require very strong and comprehensive knowledge as the basis. Most of the Internet data is unstructured data. It needs to identify entities from a large amount of data, classify and disambiguate entities, extract relationships, and build entities-relationship-entities. The most common knowledge base are DBpedia [23] and Freebase [24], which automatically generate structured knowledge repositories based on Wikipedia [25]. The technical architecture of the knowledge graph is shown in Fig. 2.

For the entity recognition task, the most effective technique is based on the deep learning method, the method based on the recurrent neural network RNN [26,27], the method based on the convolutional neural network CNN [28] method ID-CNN, the hybrid model method [29,30] LSTM-CNN-CRF. For the relationship extraction tasks, there are RNN-based [31,32] methods, CNN-based [33–35] methods, and hybrid models [36].

First, use some models for word vector representation, such as Word2Vec, FastText, CBOW, GloVe. However, the word embedding obtained by these models is static and cannot solve the ambiguous problem. Unsupervised training based on large-scale text can learn the semantic information in the data, the pre-training model solved the above problem. Such as EMo [37] based on two-layer bidirectional LSTM, GPT [38] based on one-way Transformer, and BERT [39] based on bidirectional Transformer and fusion the next sentence prediction task. The best performing model in the entity recognition task is the BERT-Softmax [39] model. In the relationship extraction task, the pre-training model GPT combined with the multi-task language model TRE [40] works best.

The limited domain question answering system means that the problem that the system can handle is limited to a certain field or a certain content range. For example, the question answering system for legal MOOC education is a limited domain question answering system. A question answering system for Frequently Asked Questions (FAQs) that composes a database of commonly used questions, such as a company-specific question answering system for a specific product.

Combined with the question-answer corpus of the previous MOOCs, after data cleaning, the FAQ is extracted as the knowledge base for the intelligent question answering system of the MOOC, which can meet the needs of some questions. However, for many intelligent assistants that do not need manual

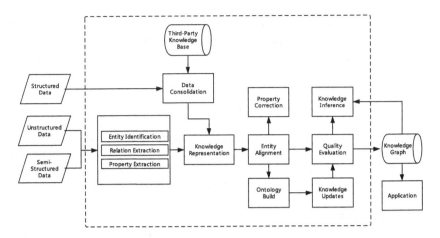

**Fig. 2.** The technical architecture of the knowledge graph.

maintenance, it is still necessary to use the construction of knowledge graph to complete its downstream task.

In the field of law, there is a knowledge graph for the case of judicial cases, embedding the semantic relationship of multi-task joints, which can realize the automatic construction of the knowledge graph of the case of 100,000 orders.

Question answering system based on FQA can satisfy basic needs, but still can't to efficient entity recognition of long difficult sentences. Most of the proper nouns in law are relatively long. The MeTa technology that is very good in law can identify the language after break the sentence down. If there is no broken, it will greatly reduce the correct rate of question answering. Entity recognition and relationship extraction of long sentences, automatic generation of knowledge base, multi-round dialogue system, and accurate location of inquiry points are all future directions for intelligent question answering.

## 4    Artificial Intelligence Anti-cheat Warning

In recent years, there has been a large volume of cheats in the field of MOOC, including the use of plug-in, hiring people to watch online classes, and taking the exam on behalf of others. This has seriously affected the order of teaching in MOOC and endangered the promotion of MOOC. It is an inevitable technical choice to remotely determine whether the learning subject is indeed authorized. A variety of artificial intelligence technologies can be used for this purpose, including face recognition and student portrait analysis, which can determine whether the learning subject is authorized.

The steps of the anti-cheat warning are as follows: First, faces are collected when students register to learn MOOC and meanwhile facial features are extracted. Second, face recognition is performed before learning or during studying MOOC, for the requirement for the times of learning is necessary to ensure that the students finally have complete mastery of the knowledge; thirdly, face recognition is utilized at the final exam. Students need to face the camera and blink eyes during the recognition process. The above identification method may involve personal privacy, and the rules of the course elective service agreement could be formulated, and the students shall determine whether or not to participate. For students who do not apply for credit, they can be exempt.

In this scenario, the face recognition technology flow is: firstly, we use the face anti-spoof detection technology to determine whether the input face is live or not, then a set of live face images are transferred to the following training stage. Through offline learning, we construct a neural network model to extract the feature of the face image. During face verification, an image is presented, and the face feature vector corresponding to the image is obtained after inputting it into the existing model. Finally, the system computes the similarity between this image feature and those in training data to determine whether the face is authorized, as shown in Fig. 3.

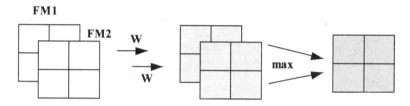

**Fig. 3.** The process of face recognition in MOOC Anti-cheating warning system.

General face recognition problems such as gesture and light variations need not be handled in this scenario because the quality of student figure we collected is relatively better. However, it is necessary to pay special attention to the ability of the anti-spoofing algorithm. If there is a cheating, it will seriously affect the class order and reduce the quality of teaching. Traditional anti-spoofing algorithm design face feature in terms of the difference between living and spoof, which are used to train a classifier to obtain verification result [41]. Designs image feature according to the joint color-texture information from the luminance and the chrominance channels, then apply Chi-square distance to compute the similarity. [42] constructs a composite classifier consisting of dynamic mode decomposition (DMD), local binary patterns (LBPs), and SVMs with a histogram intersection kernel, which can capture the dynamic information. In recent years, many variants based on CNN and RNN have also yielded remarkable results in anti-spoofing detection tasks [43,44].

After the completion of detecting spoof, we can employ deep learning techniques for face verification. AlexNet, VGGNet, GoogleNet, ResNet and SENet [45–49]. These powerful baseline networks consist of different convolution and pooling layers of CNN. Putting different activation functions into each convolutional layer, they elaborate novel technologies to maximize the depth of layers under the limited conditions and achieve high precision. Based on these major neural network structures, some new methods have been proposed. [50] presents a Light CNN framework with MFM activation function to learn a compact embedding. Light CNN model is shown in Table 1. The MFM 2/1 process which combines two feature maps and outputs element-wise maximum one as shown in Fig. 4.

**Table 1.** Light CNN: reduce the number of parameters by using small size kernels.

| Type | Filter size/stride | Output size |
|------|--------------------|-------------|
| Conv1 | $9 \times 9/1$ | $120 \times 120 \times 96$ |
| MFM1 | – | $120 \times 120 \times 48$ |
| Pool1 | $2 \times 2/2$ | $60 \times 60 \times 48$ |
| Conv2 | $5 \times 5/1$ | $56 \times 56 \times 192$ |
| MFM2 | – | $56 \times 56 \times 96$ |
| Pool2 | $2 \times 2/2$ | $28 \times 28 \times 96$ |
| Conv3 | $5 \times 5/1$ | $24 \times 24 \times 256$ |
| MFM3 | – | $24 \times 24 \times 128$ |
| Pool3 | $2 \times 2/2$ | $12 \times 12 \times 128$ |
| Conv4 | $4 \times 4/1$ | $9 \times 9 \times 384$ |
| MFM4 | – | $9 \times 9 \times 192$ |
| Pool4 | $2 \times 2/2$ | $5 \times 5 \times 192$ |
| fc1 | | $5 \times 5 \times 192$ |
| MFM-fc1 | | |

In the MOOC system, we can abstract the learning times, video viewing time and other information of students obtained by user logs into various labels or data of student portraits. On this basis, it is more manageable to further analyze and mine the data to build a useful model. Student portraits can be divided into two parts: on the one hand, describe student habits of using keyboard, mouse, and computer; on the other hand, summarize the learning states of students. In terms of habits, the frequency of using a mouse, mouse movement speed vary from person to person, and the frequency of tapping and error rate are also different, so the description of habits is a distinguishable feature. In terms of learning state, whether a student is serious or not can be judged according to the learning times, the time length of watching the video, the score of chapter test, and the learning efficiency. All the above information can be used as the feature of the students for machine learning. The students who may cheat can be initially screened out and face verification is performed specially for those students before the exam.

We assume that students who are serious about learning course are more than those who are perfunctory about studying, and they have different learning

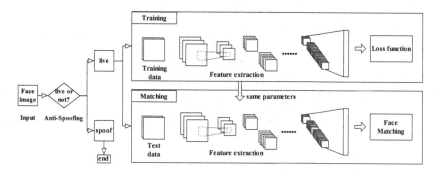

**Fig. 4.** The MFM2/1 activation function.

habits. Therefore, the dataset obtained from user logs is unbalanced and can be divided into two categories–cheat or not cheat. Although the exact category of each sample is unknown, the number of potential cheating students is relatively small. In this case, we can treat the data points from minority class as outliers and use the unsupervised outlier detection method to discover the students who may cheat.

The isolated forest algorithm [51] can be adopted to accomplish this task. We randomly sample the dataset many times and recursively divide the sampling set by randomly selecting an attribute q and a split value p. This process constructs an iTree, as shown in Fig. 5 and 6. Then calculate the average height of the sample in iTrees which is used to measure the probability $s(x, n) = 2^{-\frac{E(h(x))}{c(n)}}$ of being an outlier. If it is greater than the threshold value, it will be determined as the abnormal point. Instances with distinguishable attribute-values are more likely to be separated and have short path lengths.

Also, the SVDD (Support vector domain description)method can be used to detect outliers [52]. This method gets a spherical data description in the feature

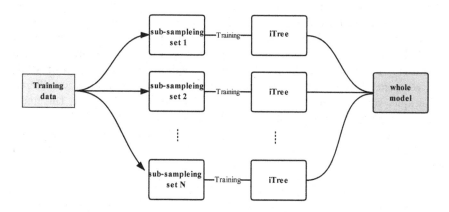

**Fig. 5.** The framework of Isolated Forest algorithm.

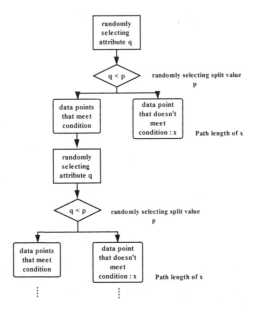

**Fig. 6.** iTree.

space, in other words, to build a spherical boundary with the smallest volume but containing as many normal data points as possible. Samples outside the spherical boundary are determined as outliers. Furthermore, one can project the data to some feature space by using kernel function to get a more generalizing model. Both of the above methods are suitable for small and medium data sets, which are proper for use in this scenario.

The fusion feature model may be considered for identity recognition. Based on the single biological characteristics like face, the recognition system can only get a limited recognition rate from the local part of the identity recognition issue. To make the algorithm more accurate, we seek to try to apply the fusion of multiple features to make up for the deficiencies of a single technology. In the scenario of Anti-Cheat warning in MOOC, it is easy to get the distinguishable using habit of a student, which can be regarded as a rough biological feature to determine whether the using subject is authorized or not. The reason for doing so is, as mentioned before, each person's habit of using computers is different and unique, such as when using a mouse and keyboard. Of course, the fusion model that integrates the use habits as features may vary greatly due to other reasons such as the replacement of computers. Therefore, personal habits are rough and uncertain biometrics that need to be utilized carefully in different scenes and datasets.

## 5   Update of Artificial Intelligence Legal MOOC

Automatic Speech Recognition (ASR) is the technology that automatically converts speech containing text information into text information through the computer, also called speech to text (STT). In the production of the MOOC, we can use speech recognition technology to convert audio into text. At present, the most widely used speech recognition technology is Long Short-Term Memory, because of the high accuracy of network recognition and relatively low training complexity is widely used in real time recognition in the industry.

The earliest speech recognition research began in 1952, and Bell Labs has realized the first speech recognition system that recognized ten English numbers. In the 1960s, the Japanese RCA laboratory solved the problem of non-uniform time scale of speech signals and significantly improved recognition performance. In the 1970s, with the development of artificial intelligence technology, the research process of speech recognition was greatly accelerated. In the 1980s, the Hidden Markov Model and Artificial Neural Networks were successfully applied in speech recognition technology.

In the 1950s, China began to research and develop speech recognition technology. Since the implementation of the National 863 Program in 1987, the National 863 Intelligent Computer Expert Group has established a special project for speech recognition technology research. The research level of speech recognition technology in our country has basically kept pace with that of foreign countries. The speech technology and special chip design group of the Department of Electronic Engineering of Tsinghua University has developed a non-specific Chinese digital string continuous speech recognition system with an accuracy of more than 90%. The best speech of the speech recognition, iFlytek, can realize the multi-language synthetic anchor through the voice query file and automatically form the corresponding text. In the last two years, the emergence of Generative Adversarial Nets [53] (GAN) has made great progress in image generation technology, enabling the generation of images based on text. A schematic diagram of the GAN model is shown in Fig. 7.

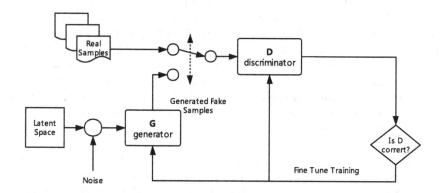

**Fig. 7.** A schematic diagram of the GAN model.

It is realized that the mouth shape can be modified by inputting text [54]. Researchers have shown in the paper that the technology is mainly used in video missed lines or missed shots, reducing the pressure on video editors, and does not require video producers to spend a lot of money to re-shoot. This coincides with our philosophy in the update of the MOOC. As the speed of updating the laws and regulations is increasing, the same law only needs to update a very small number of laws at a time, but the MOOC need to be re-created. It takes a lot of manpower and resources. The use of this technology will greatly reduce the workload. However, the technology has not yet been disclosed, because for some politicians, it will be easy to tamper with their speech.

Speech recognition is poorly robust and can be disturbed by noise. In different environments, the sound of the same person changes dramatically, resulting in distortion of the sound. Large-scale corpus annotation and analysis requires long-term accumulation. However, the corpus of the legal MOOC is very small. The current speech recognition technology can't accurately phrase short sentences, which is also a serious problem.

The characters in the picture generated by the current technology have serious ghosting phenomenon. There will be missing images in two consecutive frames of animation, and some images will have a phantom image and a blurred phenomenon visible to the naked eye. This will be the direction of further research.

## 6    Conclusion

The above discusses the application of artificial intelligence technology in the field of legal MOOC education. Different artificial intelligence technologies can improve the efficiency of MOOC production and operation, and how to improve the efficiency of learning has been discussed. With the development of artificial intelligence technology, the application in the field of legal MOOC education needs further research.

In terms of machine translation, the complete translation of long sentences is still difficult, and the next step can be studied by the relationship between sentences. In the field of intelligent question answering, the construction of knowledge graph is still a difficult problem. How to effectively identify long sentences, most of the proper nouns in law are relatively long. In the aspect of anti-cheating warning, it is considered to integrate multiple features for identity recognition. In order to make the algorithm more accurate, it is necessary to try to use the fusion of multiple features to make up for the shortcomings of the single technology. For speech recognition and techniques for modifying images based on text, improving robustness is still a very pressing issue. The ghosting of the picture will greatly reduce the user experience.

Artificial intelligence technology only be combined with specific industries and used in specific applications, it can play the role of artificial intelligence. At present, the construction of knowledge graph is based on the construction of structured data, but no algorithm of knowledge reasoning is added. The use of inductive algorithms does not allow artificial intelligence to achieve true intelligence. Most of the models are unexplained, and it is impossible to explain why such a good effect can be achieved from a mathematical or more abstract level. The use of deductive reasoning should be a weapon to break this situation.

Artificial intelligence technology is still in the inductive stage. It only uses a large amount of data to summarize the intrinsic relationship between the data, and does not realize the function of deductive inference. The knowledge graph constructed by deductive reasoning will solve the problem of most unexplained artificial intelligence.

# References

1. Fasimpaur, K.: Massive and open. Learn. Lead. Technol. **40**(6), 12–17 (2013)
2. Fini, A.: The technological dimension of a massive open online course: the case of the CCK08 course tools. Int. Revi. Res. Open Distrib. Learn. **10**(5) (2009)
3. Schrag, P.G.: Moocs and legal education: valuable innovation or looming disaster. Vill. L. Rev. **59**, 83 (2014)
4. Machinery, C.: Computing machinery and intelligence-AM turing. Mind **59**(236), 433 (1950)
5. Russell, S.J., Norvig, P.: Artificial Intelligence: A Modern Approach. Pearson Education Limited, Malaysia (2016)
6. Neco, R.P., Forcada, M.L.: Asynchronous translations with recurrent neural nets. In: Proceedings of International Conference on Neural Networks (ICNN 1997), vol. 4, pp. 2535–2540. IEEE (1997)
7. Bengio, Y., Ducharme, R., Vincent, P., Jauvin, C.: A neural probabilistic language model. J. Mach. Learn. Res. **3**(Feb), 1137–1155 (2003)
8. Kalchbrenner, N., Blunsom, P.: Recurrent continuous translation models. In: Proceedings of the 2013 Conference on Empirical Methods in Natural Language Processing, pp. 1700–1709 (2013)
9. Sutskever, I., Vinyals, O., Le, Q.V.: Sequence to sequence learning with neural networks. In: Advances in Neural Information Processing Systems, pp. 3104–3112 (2014)
10. Cho, K., et al.: Learning phrase representations using RNN encoder-decoder for statistical machine translation. arXiv preprint arXiv:1406.1078 (2014)
11. Bahdanau, D., Cho, K., Bengio, Y.: Neural machine translation by jointly learning to align and translate. arXiv preprint arXiv:1409.0473 (2014)
12. Yates, S.: Scaling the tower of babel fish: an analysis of the machine translation of legal information. Law Libr. J. **98**, 481 (2006)
13. Kit, C., Wong, T.M.: Comparative evaluation of online machine translation systems with legal texts. Law Libr. J. **100**, 299 (2008)
14. Green Jr., B.F., Wolf, A.K., Chomsky, C., Laughery, K.: Baseball: an automatic question-answerer. In: Papers presented at the 9–11 May 1961, Western Joint IRE-AIEE-ACM Computer Conference, pp. 219–224. ACM (1961)
15. Katz, B.: From sentence processing to information access on the world wide web. In: AAAI Spring Symposium on Natural Language Processing for the World Wide Web, vol. 1, p. 997. Stanford University Stanford (1997)
16. Yang, M.-C., Lee, D.-G., Park, S.-Y., Rim, H.-C.: Knowledge-based question answering using the semantic embedding space. Expert Syst. Appl. **42**(23), 9086–9104 (2015)

17. Cui, W., Xiao, Y., Wang, W.: KBQA: an online template based question answering system over freebase. In: IJCAI, pp. 4240–4241 (2016)
18. Sun, H., Wei, F., Zhou, M.: Answer extraction with multiple extraction engines for web-based question answering. In: Zong, C., Nie, J.Y., Zhao, D., Feng, Y. (eds.) NLPCC 2014. Communications in Computer and Information Science, vol. 496, pp. 321–332. Springer, Heidelberg (2014). https://doi.org/10.1007/978-3-662-45924-9_29
19. Quaresma, P., Rodrigues, I.: A question-answering system for Portuguese juridical documents. In: International Conference on Artificial Intelligence and Law: Proceedings of the 10th International conference on Artificial intelligence and Law, vol. 6, pp. 256–257 (2005)
20. Kim, M.-Y., Xu, Y., Goebel, R.: A convolutional neural network in legal question answering. In: JURISIN Workshop (2015)
21. Kim, M.-Y., Ying, X., Goebel, R.: Legal question answering using ranking SVM and syntactic/semantic similarity. In: Murata, T., Mineshima, K., Bekki, D. (eds.) JSAI-isAI 2014. LNCS, vol. 9067, pp. 244–258. Springer, Heidelberg (2014). https://doi.org/10.1007/978-3-662-48119-6_18
22. Peñas, A., et al.: Overview of ResPubliQA 2009: question answering evaluation over European legislation. In: Peters, C., et al. (eds.) CLEF 2009. LNCS, vol. 6241, pp. 174–196. Springer, Heidelberg (2009). https://doi.org/10.1007/978-3-642-15754-7_21
23. Bizer, C., et al.: DBpedia-a crystallization point for the web of data. Web Semant.: Sci. Serv. Agents World Wide Web 7(3), 154–165 (2009)
24. Bollacker, K., Evans, C., Paritosh, P., Sturge, T., Taylor, J.: Freebase: a collaboratively created graph database for structuring human knowledge. In: Proceedings of the 2008 ACM SIGMOD International Conference on Management of Data, pp. 1247–1250. ACM (2008)
25. Vrandečić, D., Krötzsch, M.: WikiData: a free collaborative knowledge base (2014)
26. Huang, Z., Xu, W., Yu, K.: Bidirectional LSTM-CRF models for sequence tagging. arXiv preprint arXiv:1508.01991 (2015)
27. Lample, G., Ballesteros, M., Subramanian, S., Kawakami, K., Dyer, C.: Neural architectures for named entity recognition. arXiv preprint arXiv:1603.01360 (2016)
28. Strubell, E., Verga, P., Belanger, D., McCallum,A.: Fast and accurate entity recognition with iterated dilated convolutions. arXiv preprint arXiv:1702.02098 (2017)
29. Ma, X., Hovy, E.: End-to-end sequence labeling via bi-directional LSTM-CNNS-CRF. arXiv preprint arXiv:1603.01354 (2016)
30. Chiu, J.P.C., Nichols, E.: Named entity recognition with bidirectional LSTM-CNNs. Trans. Assoc. Comput. Linguist. 4, 357–370 (2016)
31. Zhang, S., Zheng, D., Hu, X., Yang, M.: Bidirectional long short-term memory networks for relation classification. In: Proceedings of the 29th Pacific Asia Conference on Language, Information and Computation, pp. 73–78 (2015)
32. Zhou, P., et al.: Attention-based bidirectional long short-term memory networks for relation classification. In: Proceedings of the 54th Annual Meeting of the Association for Computational Linguistics (Volume 2: Short Papers), pp. 207–212 (2016)
33. Zeng, D., Liu, K., Lai, S., Zhou , G.,Zhao, J., et al.: Relation classification via convolutional deep neural network (2014)
34. Huang, X., et al.: Attention-based convolutional neural network for semantic relation extraction. In: Proceedings of COLING 2016, the 26th International Conference on Computational Linguistics: Technical Papers, pp. 2526–2536 (2016)

35. Wang, L., Cao, Z., De Melo, G., Liu, Z.: Relation classification via multi-level attention CNNs. In: Proceedings of the 54th Annual Meeting of the Association for Computational Linguistics (volume 1: Long Papers), pp. 1298–1307 (2016)
36. Zhang, X., Chen, F., Huang, R.: A combination of RNN and CNN for attention-based relation classification. Proc. Comput. Sci. **131**, 911–917 (2018)
37. Peters, M.E., et al.: Deep contextualized word representations. arXiv preprint arXiv:1802.05365 (2018)
38. Radford, A., Narasimhan, K., Salimans, T., Sutskever, I.: Improving language understanding by generative pre-training (2018). https://s3-us-west-2.amazon aws.com/openai-assets/researchcovers/languageunsupervised/languageunderstand ingpaper.pdf
39. Devlin, J., Chang, M.-W., Lee, K., Toutanova, K.: BERT: pre-training of deep bidirectional transformers for language understanding (2018). arXiv preprint arXiv:1810.04805
40. Alt, C., Hübner, M., Hennig, L.: Improving relation extraction by pre-trained language representations (2019). arXiv preprint arXiv:1906.03088
41. Boulkenafet, Z., Komulainen, J., Hadid, A.: Face spoofing detection using colour texture analysis. IEEE Trans. Inf. Forensics Secur. **11**(8), 1818–1830 (2016)
42. Tirunagari, S., Poh, N., Windridge, D., Iorliam, A., Suki, N., Ho, A.T.S.: Detection of face spoofing using visual dynamics. IEEE Trans. Inf. Forensics Secur. **10**(4), 762–777 (2015)
43. Liu, Y., Jourabloo, A., Liu, X.: Learning deep models for face anti-spoofing: binary or auxiliary supervision. In: Proceedings of the IEEE Conference on Computer Vision and Pattern Recognition, pp. 389–398 (2018)
44. Jourabloo, A., Liu, Y., Liu, X.: Face de-spoofing: anti-spoofing via noise modeling. In: Proceedings of the European Conference on Computer Vision (ECCV), pp. 290–306 (2018)
45. Krizhevsky, A., Sutskever, I., Hinton, G.E.:. ImageNet classification with deep convolutional neural networks. In: Advances in Neural Information Processing Systems, pp. 1097–1105 (2012)
46. Simonyan, K., Zisserman, A.: Very deep convolutional networks for large-scale image recognition. arXiv reprint arXiv:1409.1556 (2014)
47. Szegedy, C., et al.: Going deeper with convolutions. In: Proceedings of the IEEE Conference on Computer Vision and Pattern Recognition, pp. 1–9 (2015)
48. He, K., Zhang, X., Ren, S., Sun, J.: Deep residual learning for image recognition. In: Proceedings of the IEEE conference on Computer Vision and Pattern Recognition, pp. 770–778 (2016)
49. Hu, J., Shen, L., Sun, G.: Squeeze-and-excitation networks. In: Proceedings of the IEEE Conference on Computer Vision and Pattern Recognition, pp. 7132–7141 (2018)
50. Xiang, W., He, R., Sun, Z., Tan, T.: A light CNN for deep face representation with noisy labels. IEEE Trans. Inf. Forensics Secur. **13**(11), 2884–2896 (2018)
51. Liu, F.T., Ting, K.M., Zhou, Z.-H.: Isolation forest. In: 2008 Eighth IEEE International Conference on Data Mining, pp. 413–422. IEEE (2008)
52. Tax, D.M.J., Duin, R.P.W.: Support vector domain description. Pattern Recogn. Lett. **20**(11–13), 1191–1199 (1999)
53. Goodfellow, I., et al.: Generative adversarial nets. In: Advances in Neural Information Processing Systems, pp. 2672–2680 (2014)
54. Fried, O., et al.: Text-based editing of talking-head video. arXiv preprint arXiv:1906.01524 (2019)

# PYTHON Language Teaching Reform and Innovation in the Short Semester

Yan Qiang[✉], Juanjuan Zhao, Ming Li, Dongxia Meng,
and Xiaoling Ren

Graduate School of Information and Computer Science,
Taiyuan University of Technology, Taiyuan 030600, China
{quangyan, zhaojuanjuan}@tyut.edu.cn

**Abstract.** In recent years, the Python language, featuring in simplicity, efficiency, flexibility and strong applicability with rich class libraries, has been widely promoted and applied in various industries and the popularity is inevitable due to continuous development of artificial intelligence. Therefore, our school has carried out the intensive training of Python language targeting all freshmen via the innovative utilization of short semester. In view of the faculty, teaching management, supporting teaching materials and assessment methods, this paper discusses the problems and solutions of our Python language teaching reform and innovation in short semester, with the achievements and enlightenment of teaching reform clarified from the perspectives of students and teachers in order to effect certain direction and guidance for the teaching of Python language and computer language programming in colleges and universities.

**Keywords:** Python language · Short semester · Teaching reform and innovation

## 1 Introduction

After the improvement and development over nearly 30 years, Python language emerged around 1990 with distinctive features (e.g. open-source, universality, simplicity, elegance and efficient ecosystem) has become the most popular programming language in the world. The Python language generated, developed and regenerated in the context of computational ecology has attracted extensive attention due to the eco-oriented design concept and programming closest to the natural language, with the current over 140,000 third-party libraries supporting the applications in computing field (e.g. data processing, artificial intelligence, Web parsing, cyberspace, human-machine interaction, artistic design) [1, 2]. Compared with the traditional C/Java/VB languages, the Python language with rich class libraries attaches less attention to syntax and type, however it is available for the integrated utilization with other languages or platforms due to the powerful platform portability/scalability and flexible combination. More importantly, the Python language closest to the natural language has the relatively simple syntax among existing general-purpose programming languages. At present, the rapid development of artificial intelligence has turned the Python language into an

© Springer Nature Singapore Pte Ltd. 2020
W. Hong et al. (Eds.): NCCSTE 2019, CCIS 1216, pp. 38–48, 2020.
https://doi.org/10.1007/978-981-15-5390-5_4

essential part in various industries (e.g. kernel code of Google, Disney animation and simulation), thus achieving the universal application and high degree of user recognition. Most of the world-renowned colleges and universities have the Python language courses, and a batch of Chinese colleges and universities also follow the trend in practice. Learning from the American colleges and universities, the implementation of summer short semester in Chinese colleges and universities indicates the intention and exploration of internationalized improvement of talent cultivation system and strengthened practice based education [3]. The short semester focusing on strengthened teaching reform is designed to improve the students' practical application capabilities, therefore it is the best platform for Python language training and promotion. Domestic colleges and universities shall realize the necessity and urgency of programming capability improvement and extensive Python language promotion among all students (especially the freshmen and sophomores) through the full use of programming courses in short semester. The author has initially carried out the Python language training for all freshmen at Taiyuan University of Technology in the 2019 short semester, with a series of teaching mode reforms and innovations completed. The advantages of Python language training for college freshmen in short semester are as follows: (1) The society with constant progress and rapid economic development has higher requirements for college graduates on the global market in terms of knowledge structure, thinking mode and innovation ability, especially the work adaptability and practical abilities that are taken as key indicators of competence. Nowadays, the machine learning capabilities (especially computer skills) of college graduates become increasingly important considering the highly informative/intelligent development of all industries, and the Python language suitable for beginners and non-professionals can guarantee the mastering of basic programming rules in a short period, thus enhancing their confidence in learning computing languages and computational thinking. (2) The daily learning activities of college students (whether they are computer majors or not) such as algorithm analysis, structural analysis, auxiliary design and virtual reality are inseparable from programming practices, therefore the core application ability becomes the necessity for computer skills and programming application enhancement concerning the effective measures taken to follow the new global trend of higher-education development, and the Python language is available to improve the programming application of non-computer majors. (3) College students in the AI era shall have the basic scientific and meticulous computational thinking, and the Python language training can effectively exercise and cultivate their computational thinking for daily application in work and life. The flexible Python language available for the free combination of multiple routines contributes to the generation of mutilateral/divergent final solutions, thus achieving the exercised and enhanced the students' computational thinking in the learning process. Learning the Python language is a process utilizing the above computational thinking to simplify the complicated and diffused problems often encountered in work and life, and its strong readability based on the relatively simple syntax and mandatory indentation reflecting the program format/framework enables the students to accomplish complex tasks by combining simply designed routines and task in the learning process. (4) Short semester provides the best platform and effective guarantee for the popularization of Python language. In general, most colleges and universities offer one programming course only for the non-computer majors at the frequency of once/twice a week in accordance with the teaching plan, which fails to achieve the continuous/intensive learning and the students with lower enthusiasm cannot master the specialized abstract and difficult computer language programming, let alone the improvement of application skills. On the contrary, the students can master new knowledge as usual while reviewing the old through the short-term intensive teaching and training of Python language in short semester, thus improving the application ability with consolidated basic skills.

## 2  Problems of Python Language Training in Short Semester

### 2.1  Insufficient Qualified Instructors for a Large Number of Students

The instructors proficient in theoretical knowledge and practical application are required for the large number of all freshmen involved in the short semester of Python language training. However, the majority of teachers specialized in programming training (especially Python language) at Taiyuan University of Technology are not fully conscious of the current status and development trend of Python language due to the teaching of basic/general computer courses for a long time, thus they cannot meet the higher requirements for students' programming application improvement in short semester considering the lack of followups/basic knowledge/skill reserve and unqualified teaching mode/thinking concept. Therefore, the short semester of Python language training is challenged by insufficient number of instructors and uncertain teaching quality.

### 2.2  Difficult Class Organization of the Short-Term Intensive Training

The purpose of intensive and targeted training in short semester focusing on practice and application is to ensure students with different knowledge bases can master the basic theory of Python language within the specified period for practical operation and application. However, the students may lose interest in the boring and difficult programming language with fixed statement rules, strict program logic and highly stylized code, which challenges the class organization and course arrangement in short semester.

### 2.3  Difficult Large-Scale Promotion Based on Poor Usability of General Teaching Materials

Teaching materials are required for the Python language promotion and training in short semester, especially an easy-to-read textbook covering numerous practices and practical methods suitable for all freshmen with different and relatively weak foundations involved in the Python language training. The selection of a general-purpose textbook with difficult contents will discourage the students and make the realization of training objectives impossible. Therefore, the universal applicability of teaching materials is directly related to the success of Python language training in short semester.

## 2.4    Weak Foundations of Students and Untargeted Course Assessment

Course assessment designed to motivate students for active learning is an important part of teaching activities, which can be used for teaching feedback, summarization of teaching experience and improvement of teaching methods and teaching quality. The general closed-book course assessment of traditional programming design is completed by students on the final exam papers via a series of programming codes, and the shortcomings are as follows: First, the trivial codes consume considerable time and effort of the reviewers, however the accuracy is uncertain considering the particularity of programming codes; Second, the traditional course assessment "finalized" through final exams often leads to the students' frantic last-minute effort instead of cultivation of practical capabilities. All freshmen involved in the short semester of Python language training courses have different foundations and relatively weak application capabilities, therefore the establishment of scientific assessment system suitable for non-computer majors is greatly challenged.

# 3    Thought and Approach of Teaching Reforms for Python Language Training in Short Semester

## 3.1    Multi-dimensional/Multi-channel Guarantees for Faculty Quantity and Quality to Ensure Sufficient Instructors

Multi-dimensional/multi-channel guarantees (i.e. employment of internal/external teachers, strict access and strengthened training) are adopted to address the problems of insufficient instructors and unsatisfactory teaching quality of Python language training, thus maximizing the teaching effects with the students' computer skills enhanced by solving the problem fundamentally. First, based on the active exploration of faculty team consisting of internal and external teachers, our school has invited the enterprise engineers and excellent Python language engineers with solid professional foundations openly across the province/country to serve as the part-time instructors of Python language training in short semester. Second, our school ensures strict access to enhance the professional assessment of instructors, with great importance attached to the access assessment mechanism for the source control and guaranteed faculty quality of Python language training in short semester. Therefore, the instructor access assessment and overall evaluation of faculty team are conducted from professional proficiency test (written examination), trial teaching of basic courses (interview) and practice test (computer-based test). Third, our school guarantees the faculty quality for short semester through unified/intensive training of instructors, with the frontline experienced university teachers engaged in Python language teaching for many years and external in-service engineers having rich practical experience employed to provide certain guidance and reference for the instructors in terms of teaching program, teaching methods, theoretical knowledge and practical operation.

### 3.2    Teaching Mode Reforms and Innovation Targeting the Difficult Class Organization

In order to improve the efficiency of classroom teaching and ensure better teaching effects in short semester of Python language training, Taiyuan University of Technology has adopted the SPOC mode integrating online/offline teaching to facilitate the students' independent learning of "online courses" and classroom training offered by internal instructors before the "flipped classroom". The implementation of SPOC-based Python language training ensures the targeted "teaching and learning" by responding to the students' individual differences. Concerning the innovation of teaching organization and management, our school has also launched the jointly developed online teaching cloud system ("IT Teaching Assistant Platform of Taiyuan University of Technology"), which is available for the teachers' phased assessment, data collection and analysis of teaching effects, as well as the students' online practice, homework completion, immediate error correction and problem solving on a unified platform without hardware differences and software installation uncertainties caused by different computer parameters. In addition, the platform also displays our achievements of teaching reforms targeting the Python language training in short semester via intelligent/data-based/graphical means. For example, the platform records cover the students' daily learning and practice and learning path/habits/effects. The data-based display of thoughts on education and teaching and discoveries of instructional psychology and teaching behaviors summarized in the teaching process is available for sharing, contributing to the regional guidance of our education and teaching reforms. This platform reflecting the AI-based education and teaching reforms is applicable for the Python language training in short semester and other software programming courses in colleges and universities, thus promoting the application of Internet-oriented teaching reforms.

### 3.3    Textbook Preparation of Universal Applicability to Address the Poor Usability of Daily Teaching Materials

Relying on the innovative composition of compilation personnel and reconstruction of teaching materials, our school has prepared the new textbook of Python language training that integrates multiple Internet-based resources for noncomputer majors and the short semester. In terms of personnel composition, the engineers and industry experts are included in the textbook preparation committee compared with the traditional composition involving teachers only. In terms of teaching materials, the paper-based textbook of Python language training that integrates multiple online resources focuses on application skills and basic theories with numerous practical cases introduced. In addition, the QR Code is attached to each theoretical knowledge point, practical case and assignment using the intelligent AI feedback technology, thus realizing the Internet-based integration of multiple resources covering the information-oriented and intelligent online tutoring, case presentation, extensive reading and additional exercises.

### 3.4    Guaranteed Targeted Assessment Based on the Process Evaluation

The course assessment of Python language training is designed to evaluate the students' practical programming capability and thinking. For this reason, our school implements the bold reform by changing the final assessment into process evaluation based on the students' independent learning and practical operation respectively empowered by the SPOC teaching mode and online cloud system of teaching assistance; the former prompts the students' online and independent learning, with the background monitoring of login frequency and statistics of online learning time available for consciousness and initiative judgment, while the latter facilitates the students' online practice and random testing, with the knowledge mastering and actual application judged based on the staged classroom tests; therefore, a set of scientific and comprehensive process evaluation methods suitable for Python language training in short semester are formulated in combination with the students' daily attendance, group assignment and course defense. The above reform "promoting learning through exams" ensures the diversified/scientific assessment with improved accuracy and the students' enhanced conscious/initiative learning.

## 4    Effects of Teaching Mode Reform for PYTHON Language Training in Short Semester and Reflections

### 4.1    Students Are Very Interested in Python Language with Great Enthusiasm and High Degree of Initiative

All students in modern information society have recognized the importance and popularity of Python language in various industries, therefore most trainees involved have great enthusiasm with high degree of initiative and they wish to master the relatively easy Python language through the training in short semester for practical application. The background statistics show that over 95% of the students fond of the teaching mode expect the promotion in similar computer courses (see Fig. 1). The teaching assistant cloud platform of current short semester involves the code running for over 4.93 million times (890 times/person). In addition, the average learning/practice time per student on the platform is about 6.6 h each day (excluding offline lectures and discussions), 75% of the students have an average programming/practice time of more than 8 h each day (including learning and practice time), and the learning time of some students reaches 15 h per day (including learning and practice time). The above statistics prove the students' strong desire and initiative for Python language training. Furthermore, over one-fourth of the trainees are engaged in the platform-based course learning before 23:30 every night (instead of having a rest) during the short semester (see Fig. 2). The current short semester of Python language training has two phases (i.e. July 1-July 5, involving 2,612 trainees; July 8-July 12, involving 2,845 trainees), with the course defense arranged on the afternoon of July 5th and July 12th. Most of the trainees can actively participate in the Python language training during the ten teaching days, and there are over 2,500 students of independent learning on the cloud platform each day with the minimum attendance rate reaching 97% (see Fig. 3).

**Fig. 1.** Student satisfaction survey for the short semester of Python language training. A denotes the question whether the training helpful? B denotes the question whether the learning style is acceptable? C denotes the question whether the course is satisfactory? D denotes the question whether the continuous course is acceptable?

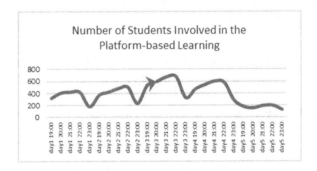

**Fig. 2.** Evening study of students involved in the short semester of Python language training. (The research data is obtained from July 1st 19:00–23:00 to July 5th 19:00–23:00)

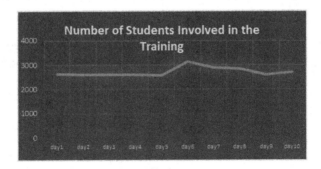

**Fig. 3.** Daily number of students involved in online learning during the short semester of Python language training. (The research data is obtained from July 1st to July 12th)

## 4.2 Remarkable Effects of Python Language Training for Students with Satisfactory Knowledge Mastering and Efficient Enhancement of Programming Application

The teaching mode reform and innovation for PYTHON language training in short semester improve not only the teaching mode and methods but also the students' learning style and skills, resulting in the satisfactory knowledge mastering and efficient enhancement of programming application with decreased learning difficulties and increased learning effects in a certain sense. The expected effects have been initially achieved during the 40 teaching hours (including the course defense), involving 5,504 participants with the overall pass rate of 97% (3,622 students get 100 points in the technical test, over 87% of all trainees get more than 85 points with only 4% of the trainees failed in the test).

### 4.3 Analysis of Assisted Teaching Effects

(1) **Non-computer majors achieve better knowledge mastering than computer majors.** The statistical analysis of final scores shows that most noncomputer majors achieve better knowledge mastering than computer majors in terms of basic theories, operation proficiency and overall application due to the intensive Python language training and offline independent learning, with their programming capability improved substantially.

(2) **Female students achieve better knowledge mastering than male students.** In contrast with the stereotype concept, the statistical analysis of course assessment shows that most female students achieve better knowledge mastering than male students due to greater class concentration and more importance attached to study and offline learning in the training process combined with simplicity and efficiency of the easy-to-learn Python language, which further proves the universal applicability and promotion significance of intensive Python language training in short semester.

(3) **External teachers are more popular than internal teachers.** The overall analysis of teaching effects between external and internal teachers shows the advantageous achievements of the former. In addition, the external teachers have higher degree of recognition among the students in terms of teaching style, methods and effects, which supports the further extensive promotion and application of faculty composition covering part-time internal/external instructors.

(4) **Many non-computer majors take the programming-related work as the future career after training.** Many non-computer majors become interested in AI after training and even wish to work in the programming-related fields in the future, indicating the great attraction and influence of Python language training among students that promote their active learning and exploration of programming knowledge. In addition, the training can also achieve the improved AI promotion and popularity, with more talents attracted to the field of programming applications.

# 5  Conclusion

## 5.1  Programming-Related Language Teaching Shall Emphasize the Practical Training

Teaching objectives of Python language training in short semester: Lay a solid foundation for the students to work in the programming-related fields such as computer software development and data processing in the future based on the mastering of basic Python concepts, programming capability using algorithmic rules, basic ability and skills of routine debugging and preliminary understanding of necessary programming development steps/stages. According to the teaching experience of computer programming for many years, the author find that most trainees cannot solve the specific problems flexibly in practice despite the mastering of programming rules and syntax. Knowledge is the abstract human cognition of empirical system that can be obtained through learning, while skills based on repeated practices are the capabilities involving knowledge and experience for purposeful activities. Therefore, practicality is an important property of skills compared with the knowledge. The skills formed and developed in activities are inseparable from practices [4]. Python language teaching shall focus on the improvement of practical skills and application capability, enabling the students to integrate theory with practice through the clear recognition/mastering/comprehensive application and flexible utilization of existing knowledge based on strengthened training of professional skills and numerous teaching practices while strengthening and consolidating the foundations in the process. The practical training and cultivation of students' application capabilities shall also be emphasized in other programming-related courses.

## 5.2  The Intelligent Online Cloud System of Teaching Assistance is Very Helpful for Programming Courses

The online cloud system of teaching assistance is an important tool for the assisted teaching of all programming courses for the following reasons: First, the students can complete class exercises, problem solving and after-class independent learning on the unified and convenient cloud platform after login without the installation of complex software, and the unrestricted locations (rather than the school computer room with fixed opening time) facilitate the students' free learning and practice on the same platform at any time and place. Second, the platform enables teachers to complete the statistical analysis of the student's learning data, batch homework correction and regular staged evaluation in an informative/intelligent/convenient manner. Therefore, the important online cloud system of multiple benefits shall be vigorously promoted in programming courses that focus on the cultivation of students' practical abilities in addition to the teaching of theoretical knowledge.

### 5.3 Summarize the Psychological Rules of Education and Teaching Based on Process Analysis for Continuous Improvement of Teaching Quality

The efficient quantitative/non-quantitative data collection during the Python language teaching in short semester has provided abundant valuable feedback information, which can be used to analyze the psychological rules of education and teaching in programming courses for the timely adjustment of teaching program and improvement of teaching quality/effects, and the teaching reforms and achievements can benefit more groups, colleges and universities.

(1) The successful stimulation of beginners' learning interest in the early stage of teaching is essential for the realization of expected effects in programming courses. Seize the opportunity at this stage to popularize the universality of AI and related knowledge and the promising career prospects in modern society before the students have access to the basics, prompting them to expect and emphasize the course study with purpose and enthusiasm; and introduce various popular contents (e.g. game programs, AI hot spots) in the teaching process to motivate the students' learning interest and initiative that are critical for the realization of expected teaching effects.

(2) Emphasize the key factor of "same starting line" and make all students believe that they have the opportunity and ability to master the programming knowledge and skills. Highlight the equivalent basic abilities of all trainees in the initial stage and teaching process to dispel misgivings because the non-computer majors have no professional and systematic programming knowledge; therefore, as the beginners of programming basics and application skills (similar to the learning of other subjects), they shall never lose confidence and be weary of study when challenged by the general problems (e.g. confusing and uncertain knowledge points, difficult practical applications); instead, they shall study diligently and humbly (rather than become impatient) to master the Python language.

(3) Adopt the encouraging teaching methods to affirm the students' programming progress at each stage of the teaching process. The instructor shall always have patience and confidence in the students while keeping in mind that they have "zero basis" for programming. For the seemly simple and even naive questions proposed by the students, the instructor shall provide systematic guidance earnestly rather than laugh or scorn at the students that may discourage them and result in the loss of interest and even negative emotion for Python learning. In order to enhance the students' learning initiative, the instructor shall affirm all their achievements openly and timely, and adopt the encouraging teaching methods for "non-computer majors of zero basis" to maintain their enthusiasm for continuous in-depth study and the mastering of professional knowledge. In short, the teaching mode reform for PYTHON language training in short semester has formed the scientific integrated teaching system covering the revolutionary faculty composition, restructured teaching materials, cloud platform-based class organization and innovative course assessment. Relying on the online platform of teaching assistance and special textbook combined with online/classroom lectures and

process evaluation of teaching effects, the student-centered teaching reform targeting the transmission of computational thinking aims to enhance the students' Python application skills through "complementary learning and practice", thus achieving the satisfactory effects of teaching reform and innovation based on the formation, understanding and utilization of computational thinking in the process.

## References

1. Song, T., Li, X., Huang, T.Y.: Basics of Python Programming, 2nd edn. Higher Education Press, Beijing (2017)
2. Chinese University MOOC[EB/OL]. https://www.icourse163org/course/BIT-268001
3. Qin, X.-Z., Liu, X.-H.: Great efforts should be made in primary school. Educ. Occup. 000.034, 30–33
4. Chen, X., Makeblock Co., Ltd.: Python API[EB/OL]. https://docs-for-mk.readthedocs.io/zh/latest/api/co-dey/

# Innovation in Methodology of Education: Big Data and Artificial Intelligence

Chunmei Huang[1,2,3], Dun Chen[1,2,3(✉)], and Wei Guo[1,2,3]

[1] Research Institute of Information Technology Tsinghua University, Beijing, China
[2] Beijing Technology and Business University, Beijing, China
chend@btbu.edu.cn
[3] People's Public, Security University of China, Beijing, China

**Abstract.** Gathering data is essential to the research of education. Tradition approaches to gather data include statistics, survey and questionnaire, which spends much time but difficult to represent the real world with comprehensiveness, promptness and accuracy, having a negative impact on the reliability and validity. However, by using the Artificial Intelligence (AI), the big data system for gathering and cleaning data improves the accuracy, integrity, consistency, validity, uniqueness and stability of research, resulting in a higher reliability and easier analysis for the data. Through the big data system, the researchers can get the data with convenience, which promote a new methodology and help achieve the goal of education research.

**Keywords:** Big data · Artificial intelligence · Education · Methodology · Innovation

## 1 Introduction

Mature disciplines are always accompanied by fully developed research methods. Researches are often conducted with critical thinking, qualitative, quantitative, or mixed research method [1]. People are becoming overwhelmed with data with the development of computer technology, which has given birth to big data research methods. It allows researchers to carry out quantitative analysis more accurately based on the increasing data volume so that they could obtain more objective and authentic conclusions and provide more reliable evidence for solutions. But is there any qualitative difference between the big data methods based on artificial intelligence and the data collection and processing which were commonly used in education? Can it bring about a transition of pedagogical research methods? This paper expounds on the significance of artificial intelligence-assisted big data research to the direction of pedagogical research from the perspective of the commonly used data collection and processing methods which were commonly adopted by pedagogical scholars and their limitations.

© Springer Nature Singapore Pte Ltd. 2020
W. Hong et al. (Eds.): NCCSTE 2019, CCIS 1216, pp. 49–60, 2020.
https://doi.org/10.1007/978-981-15-5390-5_5

## 2  Method of Data Collection in Pedagogical Research

The methods of education research could be categorized into qualitative research and empirical research despite of the specific differences among critical thinking, quantitative, qualitative or mixed ones [2]. In qualitative research, the nature of the subject is analyzed and summarized, being followed by one's own view on the meaning of things. While in empirical research, researchers put forward theoretical hypotheses and testify them with the collected evidence being analyzed with methods like induction, statistics and regression. It consists of systematic collection of information (data) and analysis with acknowledged methods [3]. The increasing usage of SPSS analysis software in pedagogy research nowadays only covers the second part of the empirical research although it enhances the analytical quality of data, but it is independent of the first part in which data still needs to be collected in certain ways. Empirical research could complement qualitative research since the analysis of certain amount of data can be taken as a basis of determining the nature of an object. Empirical research is not only designed to verify hypotheses, but also aimed at finding "new ways of explaining" [4]. The reliability and authenticity of the conclusions of empirical or qualitative research based on data depend highly on the accuracy and timeliness of the data. But what are the main methods and characteristics of data collection in traditional pedagogical research? Are they sufficient enough to meet the needs of objectivity, accuracy and timeliness? That is the question worth analyzing.

The methods of collecting data in pedagogical research mainly include data statistics, data survey and sample collection. Data statistics extracts public information or obtains data through manual statistical analysis. In other words, statistical data can be categorized into direct data and analytical data. It is common to take the data in the statistical yearbook published by the statistical department as the sample [5]. Manual statistics are also required sometimes. In comparison, in data surveys, researchers obtain data through questionnaires or interviewing related personnel as well as other ways. Sampling questionnaire is the most popular one among them. It involves the design of the questionnaire and the analysis of the results. Take the study the quality of innovation and entrepreneurship education countrywide as an example. The survey was carried out in 1231 higher schools with questionnaires and interviews. A total of 201034 feedbacks of questionnaire and 283 interview records with more than 500,000 words were collected finally [6]. Since the amount of data is too large to be analyzed, sampling can be a good choice. As for sample collection, it follows certain methods of collection and takes representative sample data as the source. For example, in order to analyze the research hot spots and trends of big data in the field of education, scholars have retrieved 184 qualified literatures with the combination of "big data" as "theme", "education" as "source journals" and "core journals + CSSCI" as "source categories" after sifting out from 184 ones on CNKI [7].

## 3  Disadvantages of Data Collection Methods in Pedagogical Research

An important method of educational scientific research is the empirical research in which empirical materials are used to testify the "educational hypotheses" [8]. The credibility of the conclusions is influenced by the objectivity, adequacy and timeliness of the materials directly. The source of the data or information in pedagogical research can be categorized as government departments, relevant organizations and individuals. Government departments have access to a huge amount of data or information but not all of them are accessible for researchers. They are published on bulletins, statistical yearbooks or others and play an important role in research. Although some departments publish the statistics, most national departments do not disclose the statistics and they seldom share the data with each other. Data or information held by commercial or non-profit social organizations is difficult for researchers to obtain as well for business or legal reasons. For example, educational institutions for children or special groups have access to a large amount of information on them but they are not public because of legal barriers such as privacy. Data or information available to the general public is only available through questionnaires or field surveys. Then the disadvantages of the methods to collect data in pedagogical research nowadays in terms of the source and access could be summarized as below.

### 3.1  The Objectivity of the Data

As the premise and basis for carrying out the follow-up research, the objectivity of the data refers to whether the information recorded could demonstrate the situation of the subject accurately. Researchers are supposed to collect data and information as comprehensively and accurately as possible. However, the existing data collection methods can hardly guarantee the objectivity of the data for the following reasons.

Firstly, the access to data is limited and only few data can be collected. The number of data released by national institutions is small and it's hard to get data from different departments, which set a great barrier for researchers. No wonder that many studies could merely obtain one type of data in one way [9]. Due to the restrictions, data that are equally relevant to research topics cannot be considered, which may result in deviation in the results [10]. There were financial and labor deficiencies in the field work earlier and they have been much alleviated nowadays. But the samples are only a drop in the ocean of the ones in reality, therefore it is difficult to be fully comprehensive and the authenticity of the conclusions is questionable.

Secondly, there are objective difficulties in collecting data manually. The inevitable data distortion impairs the objectivity. Manual input and manual collection can hardly guarantee the exact correspondence between the collected data and the original ones in mass data. It is possible that subjects reply dishonestly in questionnaires or interviews, which also causes data distortion. Take the analysis of the answer to a questionnaire as an example. Choosing "satisfied" doesn't necessarily mean the correspondent thinks so. Therefore data distortion would be inevitable if the subjects are measured only with a questionnaire rather than from multiple channels in multiple perspectives.

Thirdly, the existing data are hardly shared and it is difficult to form a thorough sharing mechanism. Although some powerful data trading centers guided by the government have been established in China, they can hardly meet the practical needs without specific rules because of the difficulty in balancing the interests of governments, enterprises and individuals in transactions caused by the lack of clear provisions in the current law. On the other hand, the lack of a macro-level sharing mechanism makes it difficult for the mass data collected by government departments and organizations at different levels to be shared and analyzed effectively and sustainably. But "deep well" of data with clear boundaries and barriers are created instead. All the above makes it difficult for pedagogical researchers to obtain data effectively so that in-depth analysis and research can hardly be carried out.

### 3.2    The Timeliness of the Data

Because the data are either obtained through the statistical bulletins or statistical yearbooks published by national institutions or other ways such as questionnaires and interviews, or being uploaded online after being analyzed by relevant departments, they are inevitably lagged and lack the timeliness. Therefore the objective situation is hardly reflected in real time. For example, the literature on the quality of citizen participation published in 2016 is based on data in 2010 [11]. And the research based on statistical yearbooks or statistical bulletins are usually two to three years later than the collection [12]. In addition, the static state of data collection weakens the continuity of the data and increases the difficulty in tracking the changes in real time. This makes it difficult for researchers to adjust the research countermeasures according to the real-time changes of the subject, which makes it difficult to put forward perfect countermeasures in real time and the availability of research conclusions is affected as a result.

### 3.3    Data Relevance

Empirical analysis is not purely quantitative, but rather combined with qualitative research. Empirical research is set between qualitative prescription and quantitative prescription and this involves the relevance of data to research topics. In empirical research, researchers need to select the right variables of which the choice would influence the conclusion even together with their "home country bias". For example, in LLSV's comparative study on the protection of shareholders' rights, the variables were biased to examine the responsibility of company managers to shareholders instead of the suppression to small shareholders by major shareholders, and then they concluded that the countries implementing common law are superior to those implementing civil law in terms of the protection of shareholders' rights. In fact, countries implementing civil law protect shareholders' rights in accordance with the characteristics of their own economic structure. Because their equity structure is mostly equity-focused, the suppression to small shareholders by major shareholders becomes the focus. In comparison, the responsibility of management to shareholders is emphasized for the sake of dispersed shareholding [13]. Therefore, researchers need to ensure the correlation between variables selected and the research topic.

What's more, an important feature of pedagogical empirical study is to "encode" the original data into a suitable form for systematic analysis, which requires the definition of relevant indicators, the setting of procedures and the basis for the assignment of original data [13]. In some studies, the values of data are quantified directly with 0, 1 logical values, scale classification or comprehensive scoring to evaluate the effects of policy [13]. In others, the answers in the questionnaire are assigned with the standard of "very agree" to 5, "more agree" to 4, "generally agree" to 3, "more disagree" for 2, "very disagree" with 1 [14]. The evaluation then is carried out based on them. But the credibility of the assignment is questionable. Is there any transition phase between the values 0 to 1? Is there a situation of 0.5 or 0.8? Similarly, is there a situation of 1.5 or 1.8 between values 1 to 2? As the number of samples increase, it is not only difficult to calculate the correlations with manual statistical methods or software, but to reflect the actual situation objectively and timely.

## 4  Transition of AI Mass Data to the Methods in Pedagogical Research

With the increasing popularity of big data technology, many scholars have begun to pay attention to the research paradigm caused by big data and even embarked on the preliminary exploration in some areas such as the application of crawler technology. The application makes up for the lack of data samples to a certain extent, but in fact still cannot break away from the pattern of collecting data in traditional empirical research. Pedagogical researchers are not good at engaging in data collection, cleaning and modeling in terms of social division of labor. It would be an ideal model that the computer experts design and complete a public service platform of macroscopic data which will do all the previous work and truly provide data services while the professional pedagogical researchers use them in the following data mining and analysis. In fact, the promotion of big data has been changing the way of thinking with the help of computer hardware and computational rules. People even have to use data to make decisions to solve the problems that cannot be predicted only with intuition, common sense, accidents, or mistakes. In this sense, big data is a resource as well as a tool. The top 10 national think tanks in the United States, such as the Brookings Institution, the Carnegie Endowment International Foundation, the RAND Corporation, and the Center for International Strategic Studies, have used computer-assisted big data as a research tool. To this end, we propose the design ideas of artificial intelligence macro big data, and explain its system implementation path and effect as well as the significance in the transition of pedagogical research methods.

### 4.1  The Design of the Artificial Intelligence Macroscopic Big Data

The big data collection process is automatically completed by artificial intelligence, adopting real-time Internet data with "heartbeat". From the bottom to the top of the data, the composite macro data of the first, second and third levels are generated step by step and the index is formed at the top level. The users will not be overwhelmed by the data and can directly focus on the key indicators. Data users can start from the top with research questions, analyzing the hierarchical data in-depth from the simple index results. Researchers can set data indicators among macro data to reflect objective economic and social development according to the real demand. These indicators are cross-domain, cross-sector and cross-structure, avoiding the "deep well" barriers of the governments and industries of data resources. Obtaining macro data then doesn't require any help from any department or individual.

Big data is generated by artificial intelligence algorithms and the process relies on basic mathematical algorithms, which guarantees the objectivity and reliability of the results. The original online information collected by the technology is taken as the input data of the algorithm and the artificial intelligence training algorithm calculate the macro data used later. The process of data collection, cleaning and analysis runs fully automatically and efficiently without supervised learning and human influence. Since the fully automatic algorithm only relies on the generated data and graphics, the data is completely objective.

Even user without professional background of data analysis can analyze the data easily with the intuitive graphical interface realized by the combination of "data stream + visualization + monitoring report software system". The relevant indicators in the system are set with the early warning function to realize the traceability of the data evolution history and predict the tendency according to the evolutionary rules of the data.

### 4.2 The System Implementation of the Artificial Intelligence Social Macroscopic Big Data

The framework of our artificial intelligence social macro big data system is shown as below (Table 1).

**Table 1.** The framework of artificial intelligence

| Social macroscopic big data | | | | | | | | Product data |
|---|---|---|---|---|---|---|---|---|
| balance degree | filling degree | | business | | industry | | | Product data |
| industry | stability | environment | population | finance | debt | business | commodity | |
| Online algorithm, Compound algorithm | | | | | | | | |
| Big data and AI algorithm training platform | | | | | | | | |
| Original data(raw statistics, raw text data) | | | | | | | | Original data |
| Script-based automatic cleaning and screening classification,LBS | | | | | | | | |
| Web crawler system(Fully automatic) | | | | | | | | |

A. **Data collection.** The data collection platform adopts the distributed crawler framework to collect the massive online information and runs it in 7 * 24 h. The crawler system can automatically adjust the interval of the collection tasks according to the data update frequency of the collection target source to ensure the effective use of bandwidth resources. The data collected include POI, e-commerce transactions, O2O, real estate, transportation, roads, website forums, social media and others. Among them, POI has more than 800 types of business categories, such as schools, hospitals, shopping centers and stations. The number and detailed name of each category are collected by gridding with accurate geographical location information with longitude and latitude. And there is information of online transactions of more than 10,000 kinds of goods in E-commerce transaction, including quantity, price and product name. As for O2O, information of more than 200 kinds of goods is collected, including quantity, price and evaluation. And traffic data include congestion of major roads while road data contain transit time, distance, toll, and road type with public transportation and self-driving as transport patterns. In addition, it covers all the available website forums, government official website mailboxes, and microblog content, comments as well as forwarding numbers in social media.

B. **Data cleaning.** It is mainly used to process and integrate the basic data in multi-source isomeric. Structured, semi-structured and unstructured data from different sources are processed and indexed into a structured format described by a unified feature set through automatic cleanup scripts. At the same time, incompliant data are discovered, corrected, and filtered, which include handling data type inconsistencies, nonstandard data units, out-of-bounds values and noisy data. The check of them is mainly implemented by clustering, sorting, computational correlation, proximity metric, local density. As for the integration of data, methods such as binning, regression, and moving average are used to smooth the data or fill up the missing so that the quality of the training sample data used by the model can be guaranteed. At the same time, it also combines knowledge from specific domains and formulation of alternative conversion rules. For example, the unified address is parsed by multiple geographic information conversion platforms and the address is determined based on the returned location information to ensure the authenticity and accuracy of the data. And the collection frequency of road traffic conditions and social real-time hot events is improved. With multiple collections of the same area or event, the real traffic situation and event development situation in the area are judged, thereby avoiding the instability of the collection source and ensuring the validity and timeliness of the data. The abnormally fluctuating data can be detected as well with the time series of historical data. All the processes mentioned above are automatically configured and executed by distributed workflows to implement batch cleaning of massive multi-source heterogeneous data. The cleaned data are credible and applicable, where the credibility focuses on the accuracy, completeness, consistency, validity, uniqueness while the applicability focuses on availability and stability. The cleaned data is categorized into corresponding statistical information that records time history on a daily/ weekly/monthly basis, being combined with Location Based Service (LBS) technology, to classify these statistics into different areas (Graph 1).

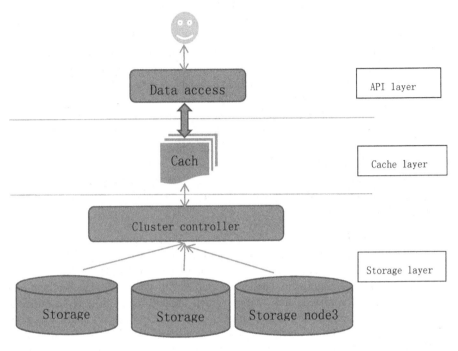

**Graph 1.** The structure

C. **Write down in the heartbeat database.** The heartbeat data generally refers to the most basic social data that can reflect the political, economic, commercial, and public sentiments of a region in real time. They are generated on different platforms in different forms all the time with the rapid development of Internet penetration and Internet applications nowadays. After being collected, cleaned, and processed through normalization, formatting, normalization and periodic processes, the data that can be further used and explored by various data analysis tools, data mining programs, and human experts are heartbeat data. These almost-real-time generated data appear in a unified dimension of description and storage mode with precise time and geographic attributes. The data collected in different historical periods form a data version that will be periodically updated and applied to the data analysis task. For example, the text on microblog obtained in real time can reflect the current hot events, social stability and public sentiment in the region. The heartbeat database provides a unified data storage, retrieval, version management, and data sharing platform, accessing all basic data, statistical data and result data in a unified format. The platform supports terabytes of data storage and is able to quickly respond to data access requests and access data to a distributed database through a unified interface.

D. **Run the incremental algorithm.** The algorithm is trained on Tensor Flow through the neural network (CNN) platform based on the basic statistical information fully automatically without effects of supervised learning or human influence, which make the process from inputting the data to algorithm results extremely efficient. Take the information of permanent residents as an example. There are around hundreds of districts and counties in the country that regularly publish the number of permanent residents. If the permanent resident population of a certain district in June is 250,000, we will match the set of the online information collected at the same time earlier and the set of corresponding population amount to get a pair of data for the training set. 300–500 pairs of such data are required. The non-linear relationship between the scale of life and social activities reflected by the Internet in a certain region and the population is hard to be found only with human brain, but the artificial intelligence algorithm of neural network can find out the mathematical relationship between the basic life information of a certain district or county and the total population. It can help to get the population of permanent residents in all districts and counties across the country. The population of permanent residents obtained in this way will be verified for consistency with the one published by statistical office. The model algorithm and data validation for each piece of data are noted in the system and provided to the data user.

Another one obtains the algorithm through the knowledge tree of the industry experts, inheriting the algorithm system of the tree structure of the experts in the industry and using the data with heartbeat to access the lowest end of the algorithm chain of the tree structure. The levels are weighted by corresponding experts and users can adjust the weights themselves. For example, to analyze local debt risks, experts would figure out the algorithm chain of the tree structure of debt risk. The first level indicators in it include the stock of existing debt, the speed of local economic development, the overall size of local GDP, the fiscal revenues of the local government, the local business environment, the active degree and scale of the local primary, secondary and tertiary industrial sectors, the number of local debt platforms and the ability of debt financing. These indicators are subdivided into secondary indicators. For example, not only the GDP in the current year, but also the average speed or average size of the past five years will be taken into consideration. There are more levels for further subdividing. Finally, bridging through our composite algorithm, the existing structured mass data will intervene and the macro-data generated by the algorithm is used to drive the tree structure and obtain the overall debt risk analysis level by level.

E. **Product data is automatically updated to the cloud.** The macro big data platform system runs independently in the cloud for 7 * 24 h with an average of 180 million collection points and more than 20 million pieces of information per day. The information is processed and analyzed every day and the result can be displayed on the visible product-side to users. The product data is directly synchronized with the distributed storage server through the cloud server and users can access the real-time dynamic data results through the product directly.

F. **Get fresh data results.** The data that the users see from the top layer is processed by the algorithm with the first-level macro data. The secondary and tertiary macro data are also available layer by layer. Each data indicator is dynamic in real time. The history can be traced and they can be used for future prediction. The data can be set to function early-warning according to the corresponding indicators. With the addition of geographical conditions, data indicators can be compared in terms of region. The system can automatically recommend similar or optimal development models for certain region and provide reference for later analysis. The data indicators in the system can be switched in one click for comparison. Data and graphics are visualized and analysis results are provided with audios for interpretation synchronically. At the same time, the system provides video interpretation of algorithms and typical cases. Thereby the first version of the report using macro big data is manually written, and then automatically updated by software and data streams.

### 4.3   The Transition of Artificial Intelligence Macro Big Data and Pedagogical Research Methods

Thanks to the cross-domain, cross-industry and cross-structure data collection realized by artificial intelligence, the data barriers among the government and industries are broken and we can jump out of the data "deep well" to see the world with the accuracy and timeliness of data guaranteed, which is a milestone in the evolution of educational research methods.

A. **The availability of data acquisition and data visualization help to save a lot of time and effort.** The artificial intelligence macro big data platform using big data technology provided by computer experts for pedagogical researchers would save a lot of time and efforts to obtain data. Neither specific sampling questionnaire for common macroscopic societal problems nor single channels are required. The system is enough to provide multi-dimensional data metrics of the social and economic development. According to the incomplete estimation, this could save more than 90% of the efforts for data acquisition for pedagogical researchers.

Besides, the traditional data collection and analysis in pedagogical research include encoding, transcription, checking of data. Then data analysis software is used to perform data statistics and testing. Finally the data or graphics are applied in reports. With artificial intelligence macro big data, the works mentioned above can be done by computers and pedagogical researchers can get the final results and graphs from the software. Moreover, the graphs can reflect the evolution of the data through dynamic demonstrations, which saves time and energy greatly and improves the output of the research as well.

B. **The dynamic and real-time nature of the data guarantees the timeliness of the underlying data and the continuous tracking of the research objects.** Compared with traditional static data, artificial intelligence macro big data can run as much as 7 * 24 h. And the data generated by the algorithm is transmitted to the client end in real time through the cloud. The data presented are the real-time updated result of the indicator and dynamic indicators with historical state attributes are available. Researcher's reference data in the report can form a dynamic report of html5 and the result of the evolution makes the research problem broader in the time dimension.

C. **The objectivity and accuracy of the data directly affect the conclusions.** Because big data has the characteristic of massive information, the source of artificial intelligence macro big data is multi-point and multi-channel. The number of collection points per day can reach 180 million and even more with the continuous enrichment and accumulation of online activities. Compared with the traditional manual statistics, government statistical bulletin data and survey statistics, artificial intelligence macro big data conforms more to economic and social operations. Moreover, manual statistics are formed in reports from lower layer with human intervention and the cumulative error could be relatively large. But the artificial intelligence big data are calculated through artificial intelligence with online data characterized by heartbeat and are better at reflecting the world. Of course, errors also exist in artificial intelligence macro data. They exist at present and will remain in the future, or rather, will always remain. There are systematic errors in the process of the generation of data but the high frequency of the generated data, i.e., the loop ratio between the data generated every day, every week and every month, reduces the errors. Moreover, the accuracy of data would increase along with the increase of the accuracy of algorithm while the traditional data lacks this adaptability and repairability.

D. **The correlation among indicators can minimize the causal deviation between subjects and data assignment.** Data are taken to seek the truth or answer to the problem essentially. It is believed that quantitative analysis is not the same as empirical research in pedagogical field since the empirical research focuses on theoretical hypotheses and testifying them while quantitative research using mathematical models or statistical quantification alone is not enough to achieve the causal relationship. It requires priori or theoretical thinking other than statistics [4]. It's difficult to reveal the correlation between data with statistics alone because of both the nature of the subjects in social science research and statistical techniques themselves. After all, the subjects in social science research are complex social phenomena and movements. Many fields are difficult to be described quantitatively and too much emphasis on quantification may weaken the qualitative differences [2]. And traditional statistics have many shortcomings in terms of data volume and statistical methods, which makes it difficult to achieve the expected goals. Compared with the traditional data sources and quantitative analysis methods, artificial intelligence macro big data could achieve one-click correlation analysis of any data indicators. The most common research paradigm is to assume that a is the influencing variable of b and use the sampled data to verify it. Artificial intelligence macro big data can find the correlation of data indicators among massive and complex data but it is impossible for human brain. Besides, the relevance is not only the judgment of yes or no, but also the result of the "degree" of the inquiry through calculation and mining of multi-layer data, i.e., the measurable degree of influence compared with the reality.

# References

1. Yao, J., Wang, X.: Analysis and reflection on educational research method in recent ten years in China. Educational Research, 3 (2013)
2. Feng, X.: Differentiation and analysis of "Thinking" and "Evidence" Methods in Higher Education Research, Peking University Education Review, 1 (2010)
3. Leeuw, F.L., Schmeets, H.: Empirical Legal Research: A Guidance Book for Lawyers, Legislators and Regulators, Edward Elgar Publishing Limited, Edward Elgar Publishing, Inc., p. 4 (2016)
4. Feng, Y.: Experience research about education: empirical study and Ex post facto interpretation, Educational Resource, 4 (2012)
5. Center for Higher Education Research of National Institute of Education Sciences, "Empirical Research on the Index System of "Forming a Learning Society Basically", Educational Resource, 1 (2012)
6. Huang, Z., Huang, Y.: The Quality Evaluation of Innovation and Entrepreneurship Education——An Empirical Study from 1 231 Colleges and Universities in China, Education Resource, 7 (2019)
7. Cui, X., Zhao, K.: Research hotspots and development trends of big data in education: a visualization study based on co-word analysis, Modern Distance Education, 4 (2016)
8. Feng, Y.: Experience research about education: empirical study and Ex post Facto interpretation, Educational Resource, 4 (2012)
9. Center for Higher Education Research of National Institute of Education Sciences, "Empirical Research on the Index System of Forming a Learning Society Basically", Education Resource 2012(1). The article states in Table 2 that due to statistics or collection channel restrictions, the rural practical technical training rate and the rural labor transfer vocational skills training rate are only used in the education system
10. Center for Higher Education Research of National Institute of Education Sciences, "Empirical Research on the Index System of Forming a Learning Society Basically", Education Resource 2012(1). The article pointed out that because the national reading rate and the lifelong learning service platform construction cannot collect the corresponding data, the indicators that also indicate the learning society can not be included in the test, so that the research results only have a "rough grasp" on the research objects
11. Xie, S., Zhang, Y.: Citizen Participation Quality and Basic Government Trust——Based on the 2010 China General Social Survey (CGSS) Data Research, Academic Forum, 7 (2016)
12. Center for Higher Education Research of National Institute of Education Sciences, "Empirical Research on the Index System of Forming a Learning Society Basically", Education Resource 2012(1). In this article, the data of year 2009 was extracted from the statistics of China Statistical Yearbook 2010, China Population and Employment Statistics Yearbook 2010, China Education Statistics Yearbook 2009, while the article was published in (2012)
13. Buchanan, J., Chai, D.H., Deakin, S.: Empirical analysis of legal institutions and institutional change: multiple-methods approaches and their application to corporate governance research. J. Inst. Econ. 10(1), 1–20 (2014)
14. Su, L., Zhang, Z., Zhang, Z.: Post-legislative evaluation method based on quantitative analysis, Theory Monthly, 3 (2012)

# Information Technologies

# Association Rules Mining in Parallel Conditional Tree

Chunzhi Wang[1], Ye Yuan[1], Siwei Wei[2], and Lingyu Yan[1(✉)]

[1] School of Computer Science, Hubei University of Technology, Wuhan, China
{wangchunzhi,yuanye,yanlingyu}@hbut.edu.cn
[2] CCCC Second Highway Consultants Co. Ltd., Wuhan, China
weisiwei@163.com

**Abstract.** With the explosive growth of information technology in recent years, the mining efficiency of association rules has become a very serious problem. The Parallel Multi-Swarm PSO Frequent Patten (PMSPF) algorithm creatively combines the Particle Swarm Optimization (PSO) algorithm with the Frequent Pattern-Growth (FP-Growth) algorithm to greatly improve the mining efficiency of association rules. However, under the computing environment of the Spark cluster, the calculation load is not balanced. Therefore, large amount of data may lead to problems like memory overflow. In this paper, Parallel Conditional Frequent Pattern Tree algorithm (PCFP) is proposed on the basis of PMSPF. First of all, through data grouping, the problem of too large a data volume to construct FP-Tree is solved. Then, through parallel strategy of the condition tree, parallel computing is implemented. The experimental results show that although PCFP algorithm generates certain data redundancy in the process of data grouping, the efficiency of the algorithm is significantly higher than that of the PMSPF algorithm and traditional Parallel Frequent Pattern (PFP) algorithm.

**Keywords:** Parallel Conditional Frequent Pattern Tree · Particle swarm optimization · Spark · Association rules

## 1 Introduction

In recent years, with the extensive application of database technology and computer networks, the amount of data increases drastically. Important information is hidden behind the surge of data. How to extract and find useful information from a large amount of data to guide decision-making is an urgent problem to be solved. In this case, data mining - a new type of data analysis technology was born in 1995 [1]. Data Mining combines database technology, machine learning, statistics and other fields from a new perspective, aiming to discover a deeper level of pattern from data, which is effective, innovative, understandable. Data mining helps to predict future trends and behaviors, making business activities forward-looking, and providing companies with knowledge-driven decisions. The automated prospecting analysis provided by data mining has gone far beyond the retrospective analysis of past practices provided by typical decision support system tools.

© Springer Nature Singapore Pte Ltd. 2020
W. Hong et al. (Eds.): NCCSTE 2019, CCIS 1216, pp. 63–75, 2020.
https://doi.org/10.1007/978-981-15-5390-5_6

The extraction of association rules is an important issue in data mining technology research. Fitting the thinking model of human cognition, extracting association rules are widely used in commercial, insurance and other industries. In real-world large-scale databases (such as the transaction database of supermarkets), rules such as "85% of customers who purchase goods A and B also purchase C and D at the same time" are found, which has great effect on the classification design, store layout, market analysis, etc. Currently, the mining of association rules mostly focuses on commercial transaction database [2–4], the attribute field of which is limited to Boolean type. As a result, it is also called Boolean related problem [5]. However, the general relational database is rich in attribute types, containing quantitative attributes (such as age, salary, etc.) and category attributes (such as gender, education level, etc.), and Boolean types can be seen as a special case of attributes. Research on exploring the correlation between various attributes in general relational, also known as quantity-related issues, has great research value.

In the past, most heuristic algorithm research was based on the application of genetic algorithm in association rules. After 2006, the group intelligence algorithm was gradually introduced into association rule mining. Alatas proposed an algorithm based on multi-objective differential evolution numerical association rules mining. The algorithm sets four optimization goals to optimize the mining association rules [6], which are support, confidence, comprehension, and popularity of fuzzy sets. The breadth of the fuzzy set represents the magnitude of the fuzzy set, which is used to optimize the minimization of project settings and rules [7]. After that, they proposed their new association rules mining method based on a hybrid BPSO [8], in which they proposed another association rules mining method called Chaotic Particle Swarm Optimization. Although these methods based on classical particle swarm optimization usually have relatively high global convergence rates, they often fall into a local optimum. Kuo applied PSO algorithm to association rules mining, proving that PSO helps to quickly and objectively search for the best minimum confidence and minimum support threshold, improving the mining performance of the association rules [9–12]. This algorithm first converts the data set into a Boolean matrix to improve the computational efficiency, and then searches for the best confidence and support by the objective function. However, the algorithm does not fully consider the advantages of using the binary particle swarm optimization algorithm. Gupta uses weighted particle swarm optimization (WPSO) to optimize association rule mining, aiming to find the minimum support and minimum confidence thresholds and extract valuable information [13, 14].

Considering above problems, we propose a PCFP algorithm for the disadvantages of unbalanced load calculation and inefficient association rule mining, which solves the problem of memory overflow caused by excessive data volume through data grouping and improves the efficiency of the algorithm by using the strategy of parallel condition tree mining. In Sect. 2, we review the existing related works. Then we present our PCFP in Sect. 3. In Sect. 4, extensive experiments are conducted to demonstrate the effectiveness and efficiency of the proposed algorithm. Finally, we draw a conclusion in Sect. 5.

## 2  Related Works

Association rule extraction is usually performed on the data sample itself. While PSO algorithm operates on a random sample S of a given sample dataset D to reduce the number of reads from a given sample, and improves the extraction efficiency of the algorithm. In typical PSO algorithm, the particles move in a direction that is expected to become better through factors such as the global optimal position, the optimal position of itself, the inertia weight, and the acceleration factor, which makes the process easy to fall into local optimization, resulting in the loss of some frequent itemset. In this paper, we propose the multi-population particle swarm optimization algorithm, in which the particles also find an optimized spatial coordinate and move in that direction. However, in the process of mining CFP-Tree, each rule represents a solution, so mining CFP-Tree is considered as a multi-objective solution problem. Using the swarm particle swarm algorithm, each path is searched and solved, aiming to explore the association rules.

Luo proposes a PMSPF algorithm for parallel particle swarm algorithm for mining association rules in FP-Tree [15]. The steps of PMSPF algorithm are as follows:

Step 1: Count frequent itemset by scanning the entire transaction database, and arrange itemset in reverse order of frequent numbers to get frequent itemset list, denoted by F-List.

Step 2: Scan the transaction database again, and then delete the infrequent itemset to construct the condition tree FP-Tree.

Step 3: Check whether the F-List traversal is completed. If yes, jump to step 9; if not, find the element's position in the FP-Tree and find all the child nodes below the element to form the conditional pattern base.

Step 4: The leaf nodes whose degree of support in the conditional basis obtained in step 3 is greater than the minimum support degree are used as the search space of the binary particle swarm optimization algorithm.

Step 5: Initialize the population and distribute all the particles to each node of the cluster.

Step 6: Calculate the fitness function value in the Map phase, Save the population with the fitness function value more than 1 as an association rule to HDFS, then the entire population is sorted by fitness function values in Reduce.

Step 7: Determining whether the iteration number is greater than T, if yes, returned to the third step, otherwise go to step eight.

Step 8: Update the particles according to the updated formula of the binary particle swarm algorithm in the Map phase. Return to step 6 to calculate the fitness function value of the updated population.

Step 9: Decode the particles meeting the conditions in the HDFS into corresponding association rules.

The experimental results show that the PMSPF algorithm significantly has higher efficiency than the FP-Growth algorithm and the Apriori algorithm, and generates more association rules. However, this algorithm has two obvious drawbacks:

(1) The construction of FP-Tree is all implemented on the Driver, so the calculation pressure of Master is relatively large. OOM (Out of Memory) error occurs when the transaction database becomes large, causing the program to terminate.

(2) Although it is a parallel algorithm, the utilization of computing resources of the slave nodes is not sufficient. The slave nodes simply calculate the fitness function value of the particles and the update operation. Therefore, the parallelization calculation efficiency is not high when the population number does not reach a certain order of magnitude. Besides, since it is an intelligent optimization algorithm, it contains iterative calculations which influence the computational efficiency, deriving from the network transmission in each generation of calculations.

Based on the above shortcomings, this paper proposes a mining algorithm, named Parallel Conditional Frequent Pattern Tree (PCFP), which is based on the parallel conditional subtree and the Partition algorithm, aiming to solve the problem that the driver cannot complete the construction of the complete FP-Tree with a large amount of data.

## 3    Parallel Conditional Subtree Association Rule Mining Based on Partition Algorithm

### 3.1    Algorithm Flow

Based on partition algorithm, Parallel Conditional Frequent Pattern Tree algorithm (PCFP) is composed of three steps. First, apply partition algorithm divides the large transaction database into N independent sub-database and stores them into HDFS. Second, mine each sub-transaction database cyclically to construct the condition tree FP-Tree and generate the conditional pattern base, then use the particle swarm algorithm to mine the association rules, and store the rules which has fitness function value greater than 1. Third, traverse all the particles and delete the repeated rules, generating association rules that satisfies the minimum confidence and support degree. The PCFP algorithm flow is shown in Fig. 1.

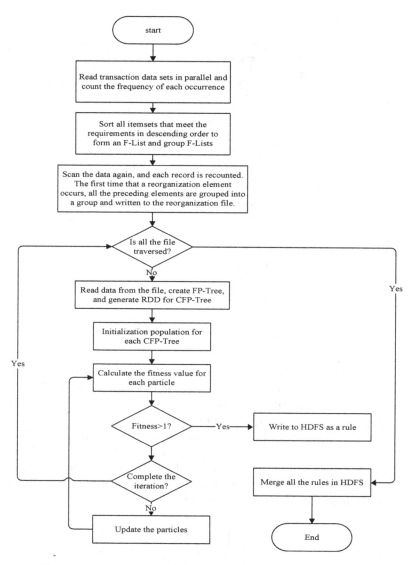

**Fig. 1.** Partition algorithm based on parallel association rules mining

## 3.2 Transaction Data Grouping Based on Partition Algorithm

In the PMSPF algorithm, the entire transaction database is stored in memory through the condition tree. However, when the data amount is too large, the memory of the machine cannot store the entire database in memory according to the structure of the tree. So, it is necessary to divide the complete transaction database into separate sub-databases.

In the Spark cluster, the step of transaction data grouping based on Partition algorithm is shown in Fig. 2.

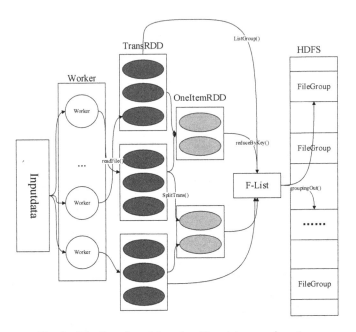

**Fig. 2.** Distributed partition algorithm data grouping steps

As shown Fig. 2, the distributed Partition algorithm implement data grouping though 5 functions. The entire grouping process is implemented by *readFile() split-Trans() reduceBykey() listGrouping() groupOut()*, and finally a large file is divided into N sub-files, and these files are independent in the process of association rule mining.

The readFile() function reads the entire transaction database from the HDFS file system into the memory of the Spark cluster, and turn each row into an RDD. The input is the entire transaction data and the output is the RDD composed of the key-value pair. Key is the row offset, which is the row-number in a transaction dataset in the original data file. The conversion format is shown in formula (1).

$$
\left\{
\begin{array}{ccc}
a & c & \dots \\
b & d & \dots \\
\dots & \dots & \dots \\
e & f & \dots
\end{array}
\right\}
\rightarrow
\left\{
\begin{array}{c}
<1, a\ c \dots > \\
<2, b\ d \dots > \\
<i, I_1\ I_2 \dots > \\
<n, e f \dots >
\end{array}
\right\}
\tag{1}
$$

In formula (1), i denotes the row number, I denotes the corresponding item in the i-th row, and n denotes the maximum number of rows in the original data. Through this function, the original transaction data is converted into RDD and is read to the Spark cluster.

SplitTrans () function use Map operator in Spark to divide each line of data in TransRDD into a single item, the output is also the key value pairs. Key is the project ID and value is 1. The conversion format is shown in formula (2).

$$
\left\{ \begin{array}{l} <1, a\,c \ldots > \\ <2, b\,d \ldots > \\ <i, I_1\ I_2 \ldots > \\ <n, e\,f \ldots > \end{array} \right\} \rightarrow \left\{ \begin{array}{l} <a, 1> \\ <c, 1> \\ \ldots \\ <I_1, 1> \\ <I_n, 1> \end{array} \right\} \tag{2}
$$

Through formula (2), once an arbitrary item I appears in the original data, a corresponding OneItemRDD of an object is output, denoted by <I, 1>, which is prepared for counting frequent itemset in the next step.

The ReduceByKey() function combines the OneItemRDD obtained in the previous step with the Key value. Once the same Key occurs, we add one to the corresponding value in the key-value pair. Finally, the times each item appears in the original data is the Item support. After that, we delete the value whose value is less than the minimum support and all items are sorted in descending order of value to get a frequent item set list F-List.

The listGroup() function is used to divide the frequent item set list into a corresponding G-List according to the user's selected group number in the F-List. <I1, I2, ..., In> is F-List, the user divides the data into m groups, then G-List is <1, (I1, I2, ..., Im)>, ..., <groupid, (I(m − 1 m, I), I(m − 1)m + 1, ..., In)> ; The key value is the group number of the group. The value is the element in the group in the F-List. The key value is the group number of the group. The value is the element in the group in the F-List.

The GroupOut() function divides the original data into N subfiles based on the G-List. The function input is also the original data in the HDFS file system, and then TransRDD will descend all the itemsets in descending order of F-List. Then traverse from the back to the front of the transaction, in the traversal each time the first scan to the corresponding G-List items, the items in front of all the elements into the group, the output corresponding to the key groupid, value for the item All previous items. Until all items in one transaction data are scanned, or all groups are scanned once, the transaction group ends. For the grouped data, the data is written into the corresponding group in the HDFS according to the groupid.

The grouping algorithm is shown in Algorithm 1.

---

Algorithm 1: Parallel partition

---

InPut: TransAction Data
Worker:
```
        Lines = ctx.textFile("filePath");
        Words = lines.flatMap.mapToPair;
        Count = Words.mapToPair.reduceByKey
        If(Words == Words) count = count+1;
```
Driver:
```
        List<Tuple2<String, Integer>> output = count.collect();
                for (Tuple2<?, ?> tuple : output)
                        If(tuple._2()>minsupport)   F-List.add(tuple._1())
            F-List.sortAs(tuple._2());
```
Worder:
```
        int count = headerNodename.length / N;
            for (int i = 1; i < N + 1; i++)
                    for (int j = 0; j < headerNodename.length; j++)
                            if (j < count * i && j >= count * (i - 1))
                                    nodeMap.put(headerNodename[j], i);
            for (int i = count * N; i < headerNodename.length; i++)
                nodeMap.put(headerNodename[i], N);
                if (nodeMap.containsKey(item[i]))
                        temp.add(item[i]);
            for (int i = temp.size() - 1; i > 0; i--)
                int groupID = nodeMap.get(temp.get(i));
                if (!groupList.containsKey(groupID))
                for (int j = 0; j <= i; j++)
                                oneList.add(temp.get(j));
                groupList.put(groupID, oneList);
```
Output: groupList

---

For example, as shown in Fig. 3. Suppose there is a set of transaction data, there are nine transaction records. Assume that the data is divided into 3 groups with a support threshold of 4. First, the support value of each item in the transaction record is obtained and sorted in descending order. Delete all elements with a degree of support less than 4 to get an F-List. By grouping, it is found that d, b elements belong to the first group, c, a elements belong to the second group, and f elements belong to the third group. The first transaction record (a, b, c, d) is sorted according to F-List as (d, b, c, a). Scan from back to front, the group output is the second group (d, b, c, a) and the first group (d, b). Until all transaction records are completed, the group is completed.

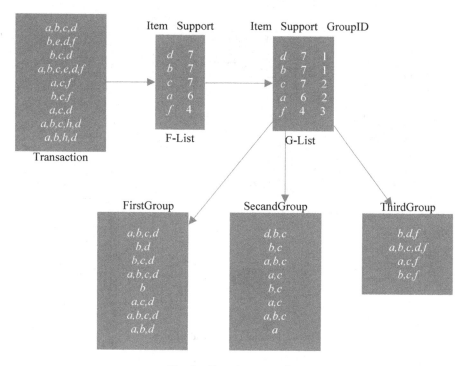

**Fig. 3.** Grouping examples

### 3.3 Parallel Condition Pattern Base Association Rules Mining

After the transaction data is grouped in the above, the problem that the amount of data is too large and the FP-Tree cannot be constructed in the memory is solved. In order to further improve the efficiency of the algorithm, the Parallel Particle Swarm Optimization (PSOPF) algorithm is improved to parallel conditional subtree mining, which makes cluster computing resources more balanced and improves the efficiency of the algorithm.

The parallel conditional subtree mining process is shown in Fig. 4.

The parallel conditional subtree mining process is mainly implemented through three methods: FPTree(); CFPTree() and psoMining().

The FPTree() method is based on the grouped files in the previous step. The construction method of the condition tree in the data of a single file is the same as that in the FP-Growth algorithm, and a condition tree is established. In the process of grouping above, a frequent set statistic has been completed, so only the packet data files need to be read once again from HDFS. For each element in the data set FileGroup, the FP-Tree is constructed in descending order of support according to the G-List order corresponding to the set of data. The root node of the tree is empty, and all the elements in each transaction form a path from the root node to the leaf node. If multiple transactions are sorted by the list G-List and have the same m first elements, then they

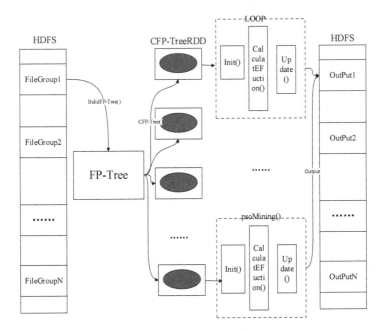

**Fig. 4.** Parallel conditional subtree

share the first m element nodes in the FP-Tree. Each node in the FP-Tree is calculated as the number of transaction sets that pass through the node.

The CFPTree() function is a set of conditional pattern bases formed from all the prefix paths in the FP-Tree for all elements in the G-List. In this process, elements that do not meet the support degree will be deleted, so as to reduce the search space. The input of this function is G-List and FP-Tree, the output is key-value key pair RDD, the key is the item ID in G-List, and value is the root node object of the corresponding conditional subtree. The output is expressed as: <Ii, TreeNodei>.

The psoMining() method uses the binary particle swarm algorithm to parallelize the conditional subtrees of the previous step in the cluster's compute nodes. In this process, all items in the conditional subtree are used as the initial search space, and 0 and 1 respectively indicate that the particle has changed items and no items. The encoding format is shown in Table 1.

**Table 1.** Particle coding format

| I1 | I2 | ... | In |
|-----|-----|-----|-----|
| 0/1 | 1/1 | ... | 0/1 |

The Particle swarm algorithm mining conditional tree algorithm is shown in Algorithm 2.

| Algorithm2: psoMining |
| --- |

```
InPut: FileGroup G-List
Driver:
    Lines = ctx.textFile("filePath");
    if root.childNodename = = P.getItemName then
        node.count++;
    Else node.item-name=p.item-name;
node.count++;
            p.parent=root;
    end if
    if p !== null  then
    p.delet.firstNode;
    end if
Worker:Input FullRoot;T;N
    TreeNode root = (TreeNode) ParaRun.FullRoot;
    For(String name: G-List)
      parentList = name.findParents();
      Path.add(parentList);
      spaceList = Arrays.asList(arg0._2);
      firstGen = PSOMiningUtil.init(spaceList);
      while(T != 0){
        List<Particle> calP = calFitness(nodeList, P,
arg0_1,allPath);
            Formula(7)-(10) update ω
            Formula(7)-(10) update particle
                T--;
                iteraterMining(np, nodeList,
arg0_1,T,allPath);
    Output: resultCountRDD;
```

# 4  Results

The experimental data that this experiment used is a public datasets, WebDoc datasets, which comes from a huge life affairs public data mining community. To compare the efficiency of PMSPF algorithm, PCFP algorithm and PFP algorithm, a set of controlled experiments is designed in this paper. In this set of experiments, five sets of experimental data were from the WebDoc public data set. The first set of data size is 120 MB, The remaining four groups have data sizes of 240 MB, 360 MB, 500 MB, and 750 MB respectively. The particle swarm is set to 60 and the number of iterations is 40. The minimum support is 0.1 and the minimum confidence is 0.7.

The specific experimental parameters and results of the PCFP algorithm are shown in Table 2.

Table 2. PCFP algorithm experimental parameters and results

|  | Swarm size | Number of iterations | Minimum Support | Maximum confidence | K1, K2 | C1, C2 | Time |
|---|---|---|---|---|---|---|---|
| 120 MB | 60 | 40 | 0.1 | 0.7 | 3, 10 | 2, 2 | 54310 |
| 240 MB | 60 | 40 | 0.1 | 0.7 | 3, 10 | 2, 2 | 89452 |
| 360 MB | 60 | 40 | 0.1 | 0.7 | 3, 10 | 2, 2 | 186851 |
| 500 MB | 60 | 40 | 0.1 | 0.7 | 3,10 | 2, 2 | 304584 |
| 750 MB | 60 | 40 | 0.1 | 0.7 | 3, 10 | 2, 2 | 467945 |

The PMSPF algorithm also uses the Particle Swarm algorithm to mine the association rules. Therefore, in order to verify the efficiency, the swarm size of the two algorithms, the number of iterations, and the minimum and maximum confidence levels are the same. The specific parameters and experimental results of the PMSPF algorithm are shown in Table 3.

Table 3. PMSPF algorithm experimental parameters and results

|  | Swarm size | Number of iterations | Minimum support | Maximum confidence | $C_1, C_2$ | Time |
|---|---|---|---|---|---|---|
| 120 MB | 60 | 40 | 0.1 | 0.7 | 2, 2 | 77794 |
| 240 MB | 60 | 40 | 0.1 | 0.7 | 2, 2 | 129280 |
| 360 MB | 60 | 40 | 0.1 | 0.7 | 2, 2 | 384625 |
| 500 MB | 60 | 40 | 0.1 | 0.7 | 2, 2 | 653792 |
| 750 MB | 60 | 40 | 0.1 | 0.7 | 2, 2 | 937651 |

From Table 3 above, it can be seen that the running time of the PCFP algorithm is obviously shorter than the time cost of the PMSPF algorithm, and the larger the amount of data is, the more obvious the time cost gap is.

## 5  Conclusions

This paper proposes the PCFP algorithm for the disadvantages of PMSPF algorithm of unbalanced load calculation and inefficient association rule mining, which solves the problem of memory overflow caused by excessive data volume through data grouping and improves the efficiency of the algorithm by using the strategy of parallel condition tree mining.

# References

1. Agrawal, R., Imielinski, T., Swami, A.N.: Mining association rules between sets of items in large databases. In: Proceedings of the 1993 ACM SIGMOD International Conference on Management of Data, pp. 207–216. ACM Press, Washington, DC (1993)
2. Gao, Y., Tang, X.: Application of hybrid ant colony algorithm for mining maximum frequent item sets. In: 2015 IEEE International Conference on Signal Processing, Communications and Computing, Ningbo, pp. 755–758 (2015)
3. Guo, J.: Research on improved Apriori algorithm based on coding and MapReduce. In: 2013 10th Web Information System and Application Conference (WISA 2013), Yangzhou, Jiangsu, China, pp. 294–299. IEEE Computer Society (2013)
4. Mishra, S., Shaw, K., Mishra, D.: A new metaheuristic classification approach for microarray data. Procedia Technol. **4**, 802–806 (2012)
5. Qiu, H., Gu, R., Y, C.: YAFIM: a parallel frequent item set mining algorithm with Spark. In: 2014 IEEE 28th International Parallel & Distributed Processing Symposium Workshops, Phoenix, AZ, United states, pp. 1664–1671. IEEE Computer Society (2014)
6. Alatas, B., Akin, E.: Rough particle swarm optimization and its applications in data mining. Soft. Comput. **12**(12), 1205–1218 (2008)
7. Alatas, B., Akin, E.: Chaotically encoded particle swarm optimization algorithm and its applications. Chaos, Solitons Fractals **41**(2), 939–950 (2009)
8. Kuo, R.J., Chao, C.M., Chiu, Y.T.: Application of particle swarm optimization to association rule mining. Appl. Soft Comput. **11**(1), 326–336 (2011)
9. Rathee, S., Kaul, M., Kashyap, A.: R-Apriori: an efficient Apriori based algorithm on Spark. In: Proceedings of the 8th Ph.D. Workshop in Information and Knowledge Management, PIKM 2015, Melbourne, VIC, Australia, pp. 27–34 (2015)
10. Gui, F., Ma, Y., Zhang, F., et al.: A distributed frequent itemet mining algorithm based on Spark. In: Proceedings of the 2015 IEEE 19th International Conference on Computer Supported Cooperative Work in Design, Calabria, Italy, pp. 271–275 (2015)
11. Agrawal, M., Mishra, M., Pratap, S., Kushwah, S.: Association rules optimization using particle swarm optimization algorithm with mutation. Int. J. Soft Comput. Eng. **5**(1), 2231–2307 (2015)
12. Gou, J., Wang, F., Lou, W.: Mining fuzzy association rules based on parallel particle swarm optimization algorithm. Intell. Autom. Soft Comput. **21**(2), 147–162 (2015)
13. Gupta, M.: Application of weighted particle swarm optimization in association rule mining. Comput. Sci. **Inf**(1), 2231–5292 (2012)
14. Sarath, K.N.V.D., Ravi, V.: Association rule mining using binary particle swarm optimization. Eng. Appl. Artif. Intell. **26**(8), 1832–1840 (2013)
15. Chen, H., Luo, Q., Chen, Z., et al.: Distributed pruning optimization oriented FP-Growth method based on PSO algorithm. In: IEEE, Information Technology, Networking, Electronic and Automation Control Conference, pp. 1244–1248. IEEE (2017)

# Ant Lion Algorithm Optimizes Network Intrusion Detection for Extreme Learning Machines

Wei Liu, Qian Huang$^{(\boxtimes)}$, Chunzhi Wang, Yongkun Huang,
Wencheng Cai, and Shuai Yang

College of Computer Science, Hubei University of Technology, Wuhan, China
1426967889@qq.com

**Abstract.** In the era of the rapid development of the Internet, network security issues are receiving increasing attention. Aiming at the shortcomings of extreme learning machines in network intrusion detection, this paper uses Antlion optimization algorithm (ALO) to optimize parameters in extreme learning machine (ELM) to obtain a network intrusion inspection model (ALO-ELM) with higher detection accuracy.), And compare this algorithm model with the network intrusion detection model optimized using GA and PSO. The experimental results show that the network intrusion model established in this paper performs the best. It can improve the accuracy of network intrusion detection to a certain extent, and improve the detection efficiency and real-time performance.

**Keywords:** Ant Lion Optimization Algorithm · Extreme learning machine · Intrusion detection · Network security

## 1 Introduction

Nowadays, the development of the Internet has surpassed people's imagination, more and more jobs have been transferred from the traditional methods to the Internet, and the accompanying network security has become more and more important. Scholars are also constantly paying attention to network security issues, and they strive to find ways to effectively ensure network security and prevent network intrusions. In recent years, with the development of machine learning, more and more machine learning algorithms have been used in network intrusion detection, and have achieved good results, including Neural Networks [1], Support Vector Machines [2–4], Decision Tree [5], Adaboost [6], etc. However, for large-scale data, efficiency and speed have become issues to be considered. For many traditional machine learning algorithms, the long training time leads to low efficiency, which limits them in intrusion detection. ELM [7] used in this paper is a new type of fast learning algorithm in neural networks. It is a single hidden layer feedforward neural network. Compared with traditional neural network algorithms, it has the characteristics of simple and fast speed. Using ELM in network intrusion detection is very effective in improving the generalization ability and learning speed in neural networks.

© Springer Nature Singapore Pte Ltd. 2020
W. Hong et al. (Eds.): NCCSTE 2019, CCIS 1216, pp. 76–85, 2020.
https://doi.org/10.1007/978-981-15-5390-5_7

Ant Lion Optimization Algorithm (ALO) [8] is a new bionic intelligent optimization algorithm proposed by Australian scholar mirjalili in 2015. This algorithm simulates the predation mechanism of ant lions in nature, and explores the search space by randomly walking around the ant lions, and learning from selected ant lions and elite ant lions. The ALO algorithm has many advantages, such as fewer adjustment parameters and better optimization accuracy. It has been successfully applied to power system load scheduling [9], enhanced voltage stability and reduced power loss [10], and optimized SVM [11] parameters.

This paper proposes a new model for network intrusion detection. It uses ELM for network intrusion detection, and uses ALO to optimize the dimensions of parameters and input features in ELM to improve the accuracy and efficiency of network intrusion detection

## 2 Algorithm Introduction

This section will introduce the algorithms used in the network intrusion detection model, and give ideas for optimizing the network intrusion detection model.

### 2.1 Ant Lion Optimization Algorithm

Ant Lion Optimization Algorithm is a new swarm intelligence optimization algorithm inspired by the hunting mechanism of ant lion hunting ants in nature. It was proposed by Mirjalili in 2015. In nature, the ant lion moves along a circular trajectory in the sand, and uses its lower jaw to dig out a conical pit to trap ants. When the randomly moving ants fall into the pit, the ant lion will prey and repair the pit to wait for the next prey (ant). Antlion's five predatory steps can be represented by mathematical models:

(1) Ants move randomly

Ants move randomly in search space to find food, while ant lions create traps to trap ants. The mathematical model of the process can be expressed by Eq. 1:

$$C\left(X_{At,n}^K(t)\right) = [0, cumsum(2r(t_1) - 1),$$
$$\ldots\ldots, cumsum(2r(t_2) - 1), \tag{1}$$
$$\ldots\ldots, cumsum(2r(t_{Ni\_max}) - 1)]$$

$$r(t) = \begin{cases} 0 & if\ rand > 0.5 \\ 1 & otherwise \end{cases} \tag{2}$$

Among them: cumsum is the cumulative value function of the arithmetic group, rand $\in [0,1]$, in order to prevent out-of-bounds, dispersion standardization is required, and its expression is 2.

$$X_{At,n}^K(t) = \frac{\left(X_{At,n}^K(t) - min(C\left(X_{At,n}^K(t)\right)\right)\left(u_b^k(t) - l_b^k(t)\right)}{max(C\left(X_{At,n}^K(t)\right)) - min(C\left(X_{At,n}^K(t)\right))} + l_b^k(t) \tag{3}$$

In the formula above, $max(C\left(X_{At,n}^K(t)\right))$ and $min(C\left(X_{At,n}^K(t)\right))$ represent the maximum and minimum values that the ants move randomly, $l_b^k(t)$ is lower bound, $u_b^k(t)$ is upper bound.

(2) Ants slide into a trap

Once ant lion determines that the prey falls into the trap, it will shave the sand down and grab the prey at the bottom of the trap, so as the number of iterations increases, the lower and upper limits will decrease:

$$l_b^k(t) = \frac{l_b^k(t)}{I} \tag{4}$$

$$u_b^k(t) = \frac{u_b^k(t)}{I} \tag{5}$$

I is a ratio whose formula is:

$$I = 10^w \times \frac{t}{Ni\_max} \tag{6}$$

w is a constant, depending on the current iteration, its calculation formula is as follows:

$$w = \begin{cases} 2 & t > 0.1 \times Ni\_max \\ 3 & t > 0.5 \times Ni\_max \\ 4 & t > 0.75 \times Ni\_max \\ 5 & t > 0.9 \times Ni\_max \\ 6 & t > 0.95 \times Ni\_max \end{cases} \tag{7}$$

(3) Catching ants in a trap

Capturing the natural behavior of ants can be described using a mathematical model:

$$u_b^k(t) = \begin{cases} X_{AL}^K(t) + u_b^k(t) & \text{if } random > 0.5 \\ X_{AL}^K(t) - u_b^k(t) & \text{otherwise} \end{cases} \tag{8}$$

$$l_b^k(t) = \begin{cases} X_{AL}^K(t) + l_b^k(t) & \text{if } random > 0.5 \\ X_{AL}^K(t) - l_b^k(t) & \text{otherwise} \end{cases} \tag{9}$$

(4)  Ant lion traps

In $P_{selec}$ and $P_{elite}$ defined traps, the position of each ant is random:

$$X_{At,n}^{K}(t) = \frac{R_S(t) + R_E(t)}{2} \tag{10}$$

Rs (t) moves randomly around the selected ant lion Pselec, while RE (t) moves randomly around the elite ant lion.

(5)  Ant lion captures ants and rebuilds traps

When the ants enter the bottom of the trap, the ant lion will drag the ants into the sand with a huge beak, the hunting activity is completed, and the position of the ant lion is updated to the position of the captured ant, as shown in Eq. 11.

$$X_{AL,j}(t) = X_{At,j}(t) \quad \text{if } f(X_{At,j}(t)) > f(X_{AL,j}(t)) \tag{11}$$

Among them, $X_{AL,j}(t)$ is the position of the j-th ant lion selected in the t-th iteration, and $X_{At,j}(t)$ is the position of the i-th ant in the t-th iteration.

## 2.2   Extreme Learning Machine

Extreme Learning Machine (ELM) is a feedforward neural network with a single hidden layer, which is one of the neural network algorithms. Compared with many neural network algorithms, it has the advantages of simple, easy to use and fast speed.

In ELM, you only need to set the number of hidden nodes in the network, because the initial weights and thresholds are set randomly. The algorithm does not need to adjust the input weights of the network and the thresholds of hidden elements to produce the only optimal solution.

For a single hidden layer neural network, if there are n arbitrary samples $(X_i, Y_i)$, Where $X_i = [x_{i1}, x_{i2}, \ldots, x_{in}]^T \in R^n$, $Y_i = [y_{i1}, y_{i2}, \ldots, y_{im}]^T \in R^m$, a single hidden layer feedforward neural network with k hidden layer nodes can be expressed as:

$$F_k(x) = \sum_{i=1}^{k} \beta_i G(A_i \cdot X_j + B_i), j = 1, \ldots, n \tag{12}$$

Where: $A_i = [a_{i1}, a_{i2}, \ldots, a_{ik}]^T$ is the input weight, $\beta_i$ is the output weight connected to the i-th hidden layer node, $B_i$ is the threshold of the i-th hidden layer node, $A_i \cdot X_j$ represents the inner product of vectors $A_i$ and $X_j$, and $G(x)$ is the activation function.

If the output $t_j$ of this neural network containing $k$ hidden layers approximates the $n$ samples so that the output error is minimal, then $A_i, B_i, \beta_i$ exists, so that:

$$t_j = \sum_{i=1}^{k} \beta_i G(A_i \cdot X_j + B_i), j = 1, \ldots, n \tag{13}$$

Simplify to get

$$H\beta = T \tag{14}$$

Where $H$ is the output of the hidden node, $\beta$ is the output weight, and $T$ is the expected output. In ELM, since the input weight and the hidden layer threshold are given immediately, the output matrix H of the hidden layer is fixed. Training a single hidden layer neural network can be transformed into solving linear systems $H\beta = T$, $\beta$ can be determined by Eq. 15:

$$\hat{\beta} = H^+ T \tag{15}$$

In the formula: $H^+$ is called the Morre-penrose generalized inverse of the hidden layer output matrix $H$, and $\beta$ is the least square solution of the system.

The execution process of the ELM algorithm is as follows:

- Randomly assign input weight $A_i$ and hidden layer deviation $B_i$.
- Calculate the hidden layer output matrix H.
- Calculate output layer weight $\hat{\beta}$ by $\hat{\beta} = H^+ T$.

The traditional ELM algorithm cannot guarantee that the input weights and hidden layer bias are optimal, because these parameters are randomly assigned. For this reason, this paper uses a lightning search algorithm with strong optimization capabilities to optimize the input weight and hidden layer bias to establish the optimal network intrusion detection model.

### 2.3 ANL-ELM

#### 2.3.1 Fitness Function
In order to improve the detection accuracy, ALO is used to optimize the weight of the input layer of ELM and the deviation of the network layer to obtain a network intrusion detection model with good detection effect. The fitness function constructed in this paper is formula (16):

$$\sum_{i=1}^{c} (1 - acc_i) \frac{1}{s_i} \cdot W_1 + \frac{1}{s_f} \cdot W_2 \tag{16}$$

Where $acc_i$ is the accuracy of a certain category, $s_i$ is the sample number of a certain category, $(1 - acc_i)\frac{1}{s_i}$ is the overall weighted error, $W_1$ is the weight of the overall weighted error, $s_f$ is the number of selected features, and $W_2$ is the weight of feature selection.

#### 2.3.2 Model Steps
The steps of the model are mainly the following steps:

Step 1: Set the initial number of iterations, sizepop = 30, search upper bound UB = 255 and lower bound LB = 0.

Step 2: Calculate the fitness value of ants and ant lions according to formula (16), and determine their populations.

Step 3: Combine ants and ant lions, and arrange them in descending order of fitness, and give the better ones to the ant lion population.

Step 4: Ant lion re-descending order to determine the current elite.

Step 5: Determine whether the termination conditions are met. If the termination conditions are met, the optimal solution is output and the operation in step 9 is performed; if not, the next operation is performed.

Step 6: Roulette selects ant lion.

Step 7: The ants walk randomly around the ant lion and the elite.

Step 8: Generate a new ant position and proceed to step 4.

Step 9: Output the optimal solution as the optimal parameter of the weight and threshold of the ELM.

# 3 Experiment and Analysis of Results

## 3.1 Data Source and Preprocessing

In order to verify the effectiveness of the algorithm, this paper uses MATLAB 2015a platform, on which 10% of training set and test set of UCI network intrusion data set KDD cup 99 are used for simulation experiment.

The dataset includes 41 characteristic attributes and an identification attribute. The identification attributes can be summarized into 5 categories: Normal, DOS, U2R, R2L, Probe. For the data of 9 features in the attribute attribute is discrete, this paper adopts one-hot coding method. For some types of sample imbalance, such as U2R, this article uses the oversampling method when sampling. Then use the maximum minimization method to normalize the data to $[-1,1]$. In this way, 20,000 are selected from the original training set as the training set for this article, and 10,000 are selected from the original test set as the test set for this article (TestSet1). The results are shown in Table 1 below.

**Table 1.** The distribution of various samples in the training and testing sets

| Test set | probe | dos | r2l | u2r | Normal | Total |
|----------|-------|------|-----|-----|--------|-------|
| TrainSet | 371 | 8687 | 301 | 104 | 10537 | 20000 |
| TestSet1 | 134 | 4421 | 102 | 35 | 5308 | 10000 |

## 3.2 Comparison Model and Evaluation Criteria

Select ordinary ELM, genetic algorithm optimized ELM (GA-ELM) and particle swarm algorithm optimized ELM (PSO-ELM) as comparison models, and use the detection accuracy rate, false positive rate, and false negative rate to evaluate the model detection performance. They are defined as follows:

$$\text{Accuracy: CR} = \frac{TP + TN}{TP + TN + FP + FN}$$

$$\text{Error rate: FR} = \frac{FN}{TP + TN + FP + FN}$$

$$\text{False positive rate: MR} = \frac{FP}{TP + TN + FP + FN}$$

Among them: TP indicates the number of normal samples classified as normal samples, TN indicates the number of abnormal samples classified as abnormal samples, FN indicates the number of normal samples classified as abnormal samples, and FP indicates the number of abnormal samples classified as normal samples.

### 3.3 Experimental Results and Analysis

The experiments in this paper are mainly divided into two aspects: one is a vertical experiment comparing ALO-ELM with ELM without optimization in network intrusion detection tasks; the other is a horizontal experiment comparing ALO-ELM with GA-ELM Comparison of PSO-ELM applied in network intrusion detection.

In the longitudinal comparison experiment, it can be clearly seen that the ELM optimized by ALO performs better in network intrusion detection than the ELM optimized without the optimization algorithm. The experimental results are shown in Table 2, where AVG represents the average accuracy rate and STD. Represents the variance, and BEST represents the best accuracy.

**Table 2.** The distribution of various samples in the training and testing sets

| Accuracy | ELM | ALO-ELM |
|----------|-----|---------|
| AVG | 0.9262 | 0.9459 |
| STD | 0.0320 | 0.0295 |
| BEST | 0.9654 | 0.9693 |

It can be seen from Table 2 that both the average accuracy rate and the best accuracy rate, the ELM optimized by ALO performs better than the ordinary ELM, and the ALO-ELM also performs better in terms of variance.

**Table 3.** Comparison of accuracy, error rate, and false negative rate of subcategories

| Attack type | Accuracy(%) | | Error rate(%) | | Underreport rate (%) | |
|-------------|-----|---------|-----|---------|-----|---------|
| | ELM | ALO-ELM | ELM | ALO-ELM | ELM | ALO-ELM |
| Probe | 99.32 | 99.48 | 0.53 | 0.37 | 0.15 | 0.18 |
| Dos | 95.64 | 97.45 | 3.87 | 3.53 | 0.49 | 0.31 |
| U2L | 98.83 | 98.94 | 1.06 | 1.00 | 0.10 | 0.05 |
| U2R | 99.62 | 99.67 | 0.36 | 0.30 | 0.02 | 0.03 |
| Normal | 94.12 | 96.07 | 0.47 | 0.34 | 5.40 | 4.86 |

Table 3 compares the accuracy, error rate, and false negative rate of each sub-category in the ordinary ELM and ALO-ELM. It can be seen that ALO-ELM is higher in accuracy than ordinary ELM, and the error rate It is lower than ordinary ELM. Among the false alarm rates, Probe and U2R, two categories of ALO-ELM, are even higher than ordinary ELM, but the difference between the values is very small, only $0.01 \sim 0.03\%$.

In the horizontal comparison, by setting the activation function of the ELM to sigmod and the hidden node to 30, the detection accuracy of each category is compared after the experiment. The experimental results are shown in Table 4, where the rows are ELM optimized by different algorithms, and the column is 5 Class identification attributes:

**Table 4.** Different algorithms optimize the average accuracy of ELM in various categories

| Accuracy | ALO-ELM | GA-ELM | PSO-ELM |
|---|---|---|---|
| Probe | 0.9944 | 0.9951 | 0.9753 |
| Dos | 0.9597 | 0.9415 | 0.9502 |
| U2L | 0.989 | 0.9882 | 0.9889 |
| U2R | 0.9966 | 0.9965 | 0.997 |
| Normal | 0.9456 | 0.9271 | 0.9278 |

From Table 4, we can see that in the Probe category, GA-ELM has the best detection effect. In the U2R category, the PSO-ELM has a better detection effect, while other categories, Dos, U2L, and Normal, can be used. It is seen that ALO-ELM performs better. So in general, the ELM optimized by ALO performs better in network intrusion detection.

At the same time, this article compares the particle swarm optimization (PSO), genetic algorithm (GA) and this paper's algorithm (LSA), and draws the fitness curves of their optimized ELM, as shown in Fig. 1.

It can be seen from Fig. 1 that PSO converges fastest, GA is second, and ALO convergence requires the most iterations, which requires more than 50 iterations to converge. However, it can be seen from the results that among the fitness values obtained after the algorithm converges, alo is the smallest, and only converges to 0.0183, while GA converged at a fitness value of 0.0325, and PSO converged at a fitness value of 0.0333.

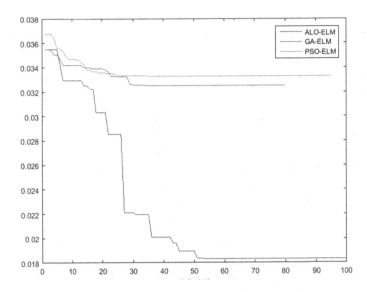

**Fig. 1.** ALO-ELM, GA-ELM and PSO-ELM fitness curves

## 4  Concluding Remarks

This paper proposes a network intrusion detection model based on ALO-optimized ELM. Through experiments, it is compared vertically with ordinary ELM, and horizontally with a network intrusion detection model using PSO and GA-optimized ELM. The experimental results show that ALO-ELM performs better in network intrusion detection and can effectively improve the efficiency and accuracy of network intrusion detection.

**Acknowledgment.** This research is supported by the National Natural Science Foundation of China (61772180, 61602162), the Hubei Provincial Natural Science Foundation of China (2015CFB594), and the Green Industry Leadership Program of Hubei University of Technology (YXQN2017002).

## References

1. Wang, C., Cai, W., Ye, Z., et al.: Network intrusion detection based on lightning search algorithm optimized extreme learning machine. In: 13th International Conference on Computer Science & Education (ICCSE), pp. 1–5. IEEE (2018)
2. Su, Y., Qi, K., Di, C., et al.: Learning automata based feature selection for network traffic intrusion detection. In: IEEE Third International Conference on Data Science in Cyberspace (DSC). IEEE Computer Society (2018)
3. Jian, L.I., Wan-Chun, F., Chi, H.E.: Network intrusion detection based on multi-class support vector machine. Comput. Appl. **7653**(1), 536–543 (2005)
4. Mingzhen, L.: New network intrusion detection algorithm based on support vector machine and particle swarm optimization. Comput. Eng. Appl. (2012)

5. Stein, G., Chen, B., Wu, A.S., et al.: Decision tree classifier for network intrusion detection with GA-based feature selection. In: Southeast Regional Conference. ACM (2005)
6. Mazini, M., Shirazi, B., Mahdavi, I.: Anomaly network-based intrusion detection system using a reliable hybrid artificial bee colony and AdaBoost algorithms. J. King Saud Univ. Comput. Inf. Sci. **31**, 541–553 (2018). S1319157817304287
7. Huang, G.B., Zhou, H., Ding, X., et al.: Extreme learning machine for regression and multiclass classification. IEEE Trans. Syst. Man Cybern. B Cybern. **42**(2), 513–529 (2012)
8. Mirjalili, S.: The ant lion optimizer. Adv. Eng. Softw. **83**, 80–98 (2015)
9. Kamboj, V.K., Bhadoria, A., Bath, S.K.: Solution of non-convex economic load dispatch problem for small-scale power systems using ant lion optimizer. Neural Comput. Appl. **28**(8), 2181–2192 (2016). https://doi.org/10.1007/s00521-015-2148-9
10. Trivedi, I., Jangir, P., Parmar, S.: Optimal power flow with enhancement of voltage stability and reduction of power loss using ant-lion optimizer. In; International Meeting American Society of Agronomy/Crop Science Society of America/Soil Science Society of America (2016)
11. Zhao, S., Gao, L., Dongmei, Y.U., et al.: Ant lion optimizer with chaotic investigation mechanism for optimizing SVM parameters. J. Front. Comput. Sci. Technol. **10**(5), 722–731 (2016)
12. Linlin, W., Jinghao, L., Xiaomei, F.: Intrusion detection method based on extreme learning machine and improved K-means algorithm. CEA **40**(284), 66–72 (2018)
13. Jianfang Y., Sheng L., Feifei H., et al.: Ant lion optimization algorithm based on Cauchy mutation. Microelectron. Comput. **36**(6) (2019)
14. Honghong, Y., Xiaowen, Y., Jiaming, L., et al.: An extreme learning machine based on Ant lion optimization. Comput. Appl. Softw. **8**, 230–234 (2019)
15. Tinghui, Z., Jie, Y., Zhanglin, Y., et al.: Classification model of hybrid kernel function extreme learning machine combining particle swarm optimization. J. Surv. Mapp. Sci. Technol. **1**, 56–61 (2019)

# Research on Association Rules Mining of Atmospheric Environment Monitoring Data

Ziling Li[1], Wei Zhou[1(✉)], Xiaoqian Liu[1], Yixin Qian[1],
Chunying Wang[2], Zhihui Xie[2], and Hongnan Ma[2]

[1] School of Computer and Information Technology,
Beijing Jiaotong University, Beijing, China
wzhou@bjtu.edu.cn
[2] Big Data Application Center, Hebei Sailhero Environmental Protection
Hi-Tech Co. Ltd, Hebei, China

**Abstract.** Wireless sensor network technology and gird monitoring system have exerted positive effects on the treatment of air pollution by providing comprehensive information. Based on its data monitoring, multi-source data direct fusion mining methods have been proposed to explain the interaction among these data. Existing methods did not fully consider the uneven distribution of environmental monitoring data and the characteristics of climate change. This paper studies the association rules mining methods and techniques of the atmospheric environment from the perspective of data mining and uncertainty information fusion theory. The association rules mining atmospheric environment monitoring data method are proposed based on Apriori algorithm and Dempster-Shafer theory together with Apriori algorithm and Evidential Reasoning algorithm. In this paper, the experiments of different fusion sequences are carried out using the data of China national control stations and USA micro stations, which are divided into the order of the first time, then space and the first space, then time. The time fusion is to fuse the rules of different monitoring stations in the same month. The spatial fusion is to fuse the rules of different monitoring stations in the same time range. The experiment changes the order of fusion to get the association rules between pollutants. Mining result representation of the mode of influence between different parameters is interpretable and practical, providing theoretical and technical support for the treatment and prevention of air pollution.

**Keywords:** Air pollution · Association rules · Apriori · Dempster-Shafer theory · Evidential Reasoning

## 1 Introduction

In order to scientifically control air pollution, it is necessary to study its roots and find out the causes of pollution in order to carry out targeted governance. In 2017, 338 cities experienced heavy pollution of 2,311 days and severe pollution of 802 days. Among them, the number of days with PM2.5 as the primary pollutant accounted for 74.2% of heavy and above polluted days, and the day with PM10 accounted for 20.4%. The "smog" culprit PM2.5 and the inhalable particulate matter PM10, which are harmful to

© Springer Nature Singapore Pte Ltd. 2020
W. Hong et al. (Eds.): NCCSTE 2019, CCIS 1216, pp. 86–98, 2020.
https://doi.org/10.1007/978-981-15-5390-5_8

human health, are formed by the reaction of major gaseous pollutants such as sulfides, hydrocarbons, and carbon oxides. Therefore, in order to control PM2.5 and PM10, it is necessary to start from their formation, analyze their relationship with other gaseous pollutants and produce conditions, to fundamentally control and prevent air pollution.

Due to the influence of weather and terrain, different monitoring stations often have large differences in data, and existing methods are difficult to find worthwhile information. Therefore, in order to obtain comprehensive and reliable rules, it is necessary to conduct effective joint analysis of data from multiple monitoring stations. What's more, how to explore the correlation and mutual influence between pollutants and to derive high-confidence correlations from complex multi-source data, which has become the urgent task of scientifically controlling air pollution.

Based on this requirement, the association rules mining model for the atmospheric environment based on the Apriori algorithm and evidence reasoning was proposed. Firstly, the association rules mining algorithm is used to mine the correlation between pollutants, and then the data fusion technology is used to fuse the rules obtained by multiple monitoring stations to improve the credibility of the rules. Through this model, the main relationship between the data is obtained and used as the basis for decision making. This relationship can be applied to the treatment and prevention of air pollution and will contribute to China and the world's air pollution control.

## 2   Related Research

### 2.1   Research on Association Rules Mining for Atmospheric Environment Pollution

In the aspect of atmospheric environmental monitoring data mining, research at home and abroad mainly focuses on two aspects: on one hand is to explore the interaction between environmental monitoring data and other events. For example, Karimipour and Kanani-Sadat [1] studied the relationship between the spatial distribution of allergic epidemics and the six-parameter data of air monitoring; on the other hand, focusing on the construction of innovative data analysis platforms that enable large amounts of data acquisition, integration, and analysis. For example, Cagliero, Cerquitelli et al. [2] proposed a data mining system, named GEneralized Correlation analyzer of pollution data (GECKO), which finds and analyzes the correlation between pollutant levels and traffic and climatic conditions at different levels of abstraction.

### 2.2   Research on Data Fusion for Atmospheric Environment Monitoring

In the aspect of atmospheric environment monitoring data fusion, the current research is more to eliminate the uncertainty of data through various data fusion methods, and to weaken the impact of different environments on monitoring data, to improve the accuracy of data and the accuracy of prediction. Representative research, Berrocal and Veronica [3] improved the accuracy of point-level prediction by combining point-level monitoring data with grid-level data, and obtained useful conclusions; Friberg, Chang et al. [4] studied the gradient of urban pollutants and used uncertainty estimation methods for data fusion modeling. Finally, the pollution concentration data with less error than the observed data is obtained. Qian Yixin [5] proposed a multi-integration framework, which effectively improved the knowledge acquisition ability of environmental monitoring big data.

### 2.3    Research on Data Fusion and Association Rules Mining Technology

There are also some researches on the application of data fusion technology and association rules mining technology. For example, Liao, Chen et al. [6] used structured learning methods to study the causal relationship between security risks, and calculated the weights of each relationship according to the association rules. Finally, the causal relationship and weight were merged to form a dangerous association network. On this basis, the source of danger is identified and the strategic planning of safety management is carried out. Guder and Cicekli [7] applied two techniques to the field of event recognition, and proposed a multimodal event recognition framework based on feature fusion and decision fusion to improve the accuracy of event recognition. The proposed framework is also applicable to new event type integration.

On the whole, in the aspect of mining the association rules of atmospheric environment monitoring data, there are few studies on the mining of atmospheric environment monitoring data and the fusion of rules, which is necessary for research.

### 2.4    Apriori Algorithm

The Apriori algorithm was proposed by Agrawal and Srikant [8] in 1994 as a frequent itemset mining and association rules learning algorithm for transactional databases. Frequent itemsets determined by the Apriori algorithm can be used to determine association rules that highlight general trends in the database.

In this paper, the appropriate mining range is selected in the original data, which sets association rule mining for each data by the Apriori algorithm and then obtains accurate mining results within a certain range.

**Mining Strong Rules of a Single Set by the Apriori Algorithm.**
*Step 1: Get frequent k item sets by self-joining, then build frequent itemsets.* Let the six-parameter data of a monitoring station be a set Ti (i for the month), then define the minimum support *MinSup*.

After standardizing the data, the candidate set *Ti* is analyzed, all the first-order items appearing are stored in the item set $C_1$, and $Ck - 1$ is self-joined. A set of candidate k item sets is generated and stored in the item set $Ck$. Store the calculated frequent items in the frequent the itemset $Xi$.

*Step 2: Calculate the association rules, then get a strong association rule set.* Define the minimum confidence *MinConf*, the mined rules are stored in the set *Ri* (i stands for the month), and Ri includes the rules and the confidence of the rules. First, for each frequent the itemset $X$, all non-empty true subsets $S$ are generated; then a strong rule $S \rightarrow (X - S)$ is output for each non-empty true subset $S$.

## 2.5    D-S Theory

The Dempster–Shafer (D-S) theory is a common framework for uncertainty reasoning, which was first proposed by Arthur P. Dempster in the context of statistical inference in 1967, and then Glenn Shafer [9] developed it into a general framework for uncertainty cognitive modeling. The D-S evidence theory is generalized by subjective Bayesian theory, but it can directly express "uncertainty" and "don't know" and has fewer conditional constraints than Bayesian theory.

The D-S theory fuses the strong association rule sets of different data sources, and the order is also divided into time first fusion and then spatial fusion together with spatial first fusion and then time fusion.

The sets of rules Ri includes the rule r and the confidence $conf(r)$. Then let $Bel(r) = conf(r)$. Thus different months as different sources of evidence, rule sets as the basic probability distribution function of each evidence source, can use the D-S evidence theory framework to carry out data fusion between rules [10]. However, due to the differences in the data of different months, even after the minimum threshold pruning process, the rule sets obtained by mining also have differences. D-S evidence theory requires different data sources to make a credibility analysis of the same hypothesis [11], so define $R' = U_{i=1}^{N} R_i$ using the formula $\text{Conf}(R_k) = 0$ if $R_k \notin R'$ for completing the missing rules in each ruleset.

Taking into account the data characteristics, the combination of rule formula (1) of murphy rule [12] is used to carry out the reliability fusion between pieces of evidence, which can deal with the current contradiction well.

The resulting set of time fusion rules $R$ includes the rule *rule* and the confidence *conf*.

$$Bel_M(A) = \frac{1}{2}[Bel_1(A) + Bel_2(A)] \tag{1}$$

## 2.6    ER Algorithm

The Evidential Reasoning (ER) algorithm, also known as the evidence theory method, is aimed at the problem that the D-S framework will have low credibility in the case of high evidence source conflicts. It was an uncertainty assessment method proposed by Yang Jianbo and others from the University of Manchester in the 1980s and constantly improved. The method involves a variety of disciplines and theories and has been widely used in dealing with deterministic and uncertain problems [13].

There are two layers of integration in the fusion of basic rules: time fusion and spatial fusion.

**The convergence of rules for different months of the same monitoring site.** First define $N$ sets of basic rules that need to be fused $E = e1, e2,..., en, e\{.\}$ to the resulting set of association rules, including $e\{.\}.rule.$ and confidence $e\{.\}(rule).con\ f$, and determine the relative weight of each basic attribute $W = \{w_1, w_2, ..., w_n\}$. The weight of each monitoring station rules set is defined as $w_i = 1/n$.

In the same month, different monitoring site rule fusion systems define $M$ mutually exclusive evaluation levels $H = \{h_1, h_2, ..., h_m\}$.

After calculating the probability assignment functions of multiple basic attributes, the results of the M basic attributes $e11 \oplus e12 \oplus e13 \oplus e14 \oplus$ that need to be merged are calculated, wherein the scale factor $K$ reflects the degree of conflict between a lot of evidence [14]. After all M estimates are aggregated, normalization is performed to obtain the final combined trust $S(e) = (hm, \beta m,i)$, $m = 1, ..., M$ and $\beta H$.

**The convergence of rules for different months of the same monitoring station type.** The difference with the time fusion framework is that spatial fusion is fusion at the spatial level, which aggregates different spatial results at the same time. Time fusion is fusion at the time level, which aggregates the results of different times at the same place.

## 3    Data Preprocessing

### 3.1    Data Source

All the data in this paper comes from the network, which is the historical air pollution monitoring data from Xinxiang, China and from Portland, USA. The data structure as shown in Table 1. The main attribute used to verify the model are the six-parameter data which is the concentration values of the six indicators of CO, NO2, SO2, O3, PM2.5, and PM10. The six-parameter data concentration monitoring specifications at home and abroad are shown in Table 2.

**Table 1.**  Experimental data resource

| Station type | Number | Monitoring item | Time interval | Total number | Data period |
|---|---|---|---|---|---|
| Microstation (USA) | 2 | CO, NO$_2$, SO$_2$, O$_3$, PM$_{2.5}$, PM$_{10}$ | per hour | 7993 | 2018.12.19–2019.6.18 |
| National Control Station (China) | 4 | CO, NO$_2$, SO$_2$, O$_3$, PM$_{2.5}$, PM$_{10}$ | per hour | 15000 | 2018.1.1–2018.5.31 |

**Table 2.** Six-parameter concentration monitoring specifications

| Type of pollutant | Unit | Actual data range (China) | Actual data range (USA) | Evaluation of excellent range |
|---|---|---|---|---|
| CO | mg/m³ | [0.1, 8.2] | [0.3,0.5] | [0,1000] |
| NO$_2$ | μg/m³ | [2.0, 313.0] | [308.62,1154.43] | [0,200] |
| SO$_2$ | μg/m³ | [1.0, 474.0] | [8.1,1559.93] | [0,150] |
| O$_3$ | μg/m³ | [1.0, 265.0] | [733.61,1376.75] | [0,160] |
| PM$_{2.5}$ | μg/m³ | [4.0, 476.0] | [0,82.14] | [0,35] |
| PM$_{10}$ | μg/m³ | [5.0, 957.0] | [0,108.48] | [0,50] |

## 3.2 Data Processing

**Data Standardization.** The experimental data values are not evenly distributed in time series as the value span is larger and more distributed. Thus, in addition to data cleaning, such as removing null values, it is necessary to standardize the data before the rules are mined.

The statistics result show that the distribution image of pollutants SO2 in China's monitoring station shows a log-normal distribution trend within five months. Therefore, the logarithm of the data can be followed by normal distribution function fitting. Finally the probability density function of the concentration distribution is obtained. Through many experiments, it is concluded that in the atmospheric environment monitoring data experiment, the sample separation span with better rule number and distribution is 15%, and the overall data span is segmented according to 15%. By looking up the standard normal distribution probability table, the corresponding segmentation value is obtained, which is brought into the probability distribution function, and the parameter concentration segmentation result is obtained, which is divided into the probability distribution function. Each partition takes the median as the normalized value of the data segment and then normalizes all the data according to its range. The representative values of each segment after segmentation can be seen in Table 3 and Table 4.

**Table 3.** Standardized concentration segment representative value (USA)

|  | PM$_{10}$ | PM$_{2.5}$ | SO$_2$ | NO$_2$ | CO | O$_3$ |
|---|---|---|---|---|---|---|
| 1 | 0.5 | 0.4 | 284.0 | 534.9 | 0.37 | 836.7 |
| 2 | 1.5 | 1.3 | 595.5 | 792.8 | 0.38 | 970.8 |
| 3 | 2.7 | 2.2 | 652.7 | 843.1 | 0.39 | 1020.1 |
| 4 | 3.9 | 3.3 | 694.4 | 878.7 | 0.39 | 1054.5 |
| 5 | 5.7 | 4.8 | 735.5 | 913.2 | 0.40 | 1087.5 |
| 6 | 8.5 | 7.1 | 782.6 | 951.9 | 0.40 | 1124.3 |
| 7 | 16.1 | 13.4 | 859.9 | 1013.4 | 0.41 | 1182.2 |
| 8 | 65.2 | 50.2 | 1234.6 | 1104.2 | 0.48 | 1298.4 |

**Table 4.** Standardized concentration segment representative value (China)

|   | $PM_{10}$ | $PM_{2.5}$ | $SO_2$ | $NO_2$ | CO | $O_3$ |
|---|---|---|---|---|---|---|
| 1 | 24.4 | 11.4 | 3.8 | 9.2 | 0.4 | 4.5 |
| 2 | 56.5 | 25.5 | 8.8 | 21.2 | 0.8 | 13.4 |
| 3 | 79.2 | 37.9 | 12.9 | 30.0 | 1.0 | 24.4 |
| 4 | 100.2 | 49.9 | 16.9 | 38.1 | 1.2 | 37.5 |
| 5 | 124.9 | 64.7 | 21.7 | 47.7 | 1.4 | 56.4 |
| 6 | 158.6 | 85.9 | 28.5 | 60.9 | 1.7 | 88.0 |
| 7 | 230.4 | 133.9 | 43.8 | 89.1 | 2.2 | 180.1 |
| 8 | 619.6 | 322.6 | 264.5 | 211.3 | 5.4 | 258.4 |

## 4   Discussion

### 4.1   Association Rules Mining Results Based on the Apriori Algorithm and D-S Evidence Theory

Before the association rule mining, since the concentration values of each parameter are all digital values, to avoid confusion during the rule mining process, the data is marked to indicate that the values of PM10, PM2.5, SO2, NO2, CO, O3 are respectively added before on the A, B, C, D, E, F to distinguish. For example, C25 represents an SO2 concentration of 25 µg/m3. The first is to perform association rule mining on the data of a monitoring site for a single month and obtain an association rule data set containing rules and confidence. The storage format is (rule item set, pre-term, post-item, confidence), such as a confidence level of 0.5. Rule A $\Rightarrow$ B is represented in the association rule data set ((A, B), A, B, 0.5). Because the mined rule set needs to be merged again, and there are many items, so to minimize the loss of information, the minimum support MinSup and the minimum confidence MinConf do not set the minimum value, discard unless the value approaches zero. Each monitoring station excavates a set of association rules for each month. There are a total of twenty association rules in the five months of the four monitoring stations in China. There are fourteen association rules in the seven months of the two monitoring stations from USA.

**Time-Space Fusion Based on D-S Theory.** The D-S theory is used to fuse the rule sets. The first step is time fusion which is the rule set of each site is merged for several months. The second step is space fusion which carries out the monthly fusion of each station first, then the result of the fusion of the remaining months.

After the fusion of time dimensions, the rule data sets of five months of integration in the four monitoring stations in China and the rule data sets of seven months in two foreign monitoring stations are obtained. The spatial fusion of the four domestic rule sets and the foreign two rule sets through the D-S method is respectively carried out. The rules for ranking the top ten of the results of the fusion of two cities' results are shown in Tables 5 and 6.It should be noted time-Space means fusion order is time first then space. In contract, Space-Time is space first then time.

**Table 5.** Top ten rules of time-space fusion by D-S theory (China)

|    | Rules | Confidence |
|----|-------|------------|
| 1  | $O_3$:13.4, $NO_2$:89.1 | 0.0375 |
| 2  | $NO_2$:89.1, $O_3$:13.4 | 0.0357 |
| 3  | $NO_2$:21.2, $O_3$:88.0 | 0.0342 |
| 4  | $PM_{10}$:230.4, $PM_{2.5}$:133.9 | 0.0309 |
| 5  | $PM_{2.5}$:133.9, $PM_{10}$:230.4 | 0.0278 |
| 6  | $PM_{2.5}$:49.9, CO:1.18 | 0.0249 |
| 7  | $PM_{10}$:158.6, $PM_{2.5}$:133.9 | 0.0207 |
| 8  | CO:1.18, $PM_{2.5}$:49.9 | 0.0203 |
| 9  | $PM_{2.5}$:322.6, $PM_{10}$:230.4 | 0.0203 |
| 10 | $O_3$:88.0, $NO_2$:21.2 | 0.0201 |

**Table 6.** Top ten rules of time-space fusion by D-S theory (USA)

|    | Rules | Confidence |
|----|-------|------------|
| 1  | SO2:595.5, CO:0.39 | 0.01051 |
| 2  | PM2.5:3.31, PM10:3.9 | 0.00985 |
| 3  | NO2:878.7, CO:0.39 | 0.00984 |
| 4  | PM10:3.9, PM2.5:3.31 | 0.00940 |
| 5  | PM2.5:1.31, PM10:1.5 | 0.00938 |
| 6  | PM10:1.5, PM2.5:1.31 | 0.00879 |
| 7  | SO2:652.7, NO2:843.1, O3:970.8, CO:0.39 | 0.00853 |
| 8  | PM2.5:13.41, PM10:16.1 | 0.00853 |
| 9  | PM10:16.1, PM2.5:13.41 | 0.00849 |
| 10 | O3:970.8, NO2:843.1, CO:0.39, SO2:652.7 | 0.00840 |

Analyzing these ten rules, it can be clearly seen that through spatial fusion, the main rules of wide coverage are extracted. Rules with the only sporadicity have lower confidence in the overall results. Statistics on the number of rules related to the six parameters in the final fusion rule set are obtained in Fig. 1. The column shape in the figure represents the number of the first few parameters in each of the parameters, it can be clearly seen that the number of rules related to PM10, PM2.5, CO, O3 is more than the number of rules related to SO2, NO2, indicating that the first four items are affected and change more than the last two.

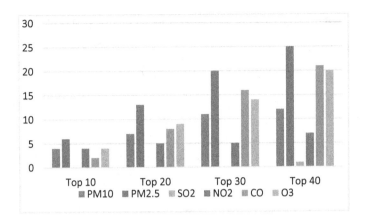

**Fig. 1.** Number of rules relating to each parameters after D-S time-space fusion (China)

It can be seen from Fig. 2, the ratio of NO2, SO2, PM2.5, and PM10 in the first ten rules foreign data is relatively small. After the scope of the rule becomes larger, the number of rules of PM10 increases significantly, and PM2.5 still maintains a small proportion, So PM10 may be more susceptible, PM2.5 will be more stable.

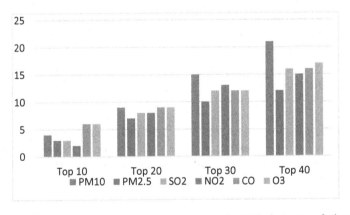

**Fig. 2.** Number of rules relating to each parameters after D-S time-space fusion (USA)

**Space-Time Fusion Based on D-S Theory.** To solve the situation that the rules may conflict from the model level, considering the actual situation of the data, the model in this section proposes the framework of space fusion after time fusion in the process of rules fusion. To verify the effectiveness of the model in solving this problem, this paper also made a comparative experiment of time fusion after spatial fusion to verify the pros and cons of the model. After the single-month rule mining of the single-monitoring station on the standardized data set, 20 rule data sets are obtained for each of the four monitoring stations from China and 14 rule data sets for each of the two monitoring stations from USA. Firstly, spatial fusion is carried out, that is, the sets of several monitoring stations in the same month at home and abroad are merged respectively, then merge the obtained monthly rule sets into time to obtain the final fusion result, and finally the rules of the top ten results of the fusion of two cities results are shown in Tables 7 and 8.

**Table 7.** Top Ten Rules of Space-Time Fusion by D-S theory (China and USA)

|    | Rules (China) | Confidence | Rules (USA) | Confidence |
|----|---------------|------------|-------------|------------|
| 1  | O3:13.4, NO2:89.1 | 0.0580 | PM10:5.7, PM2.5:4.77 | 0.02053 |
| 2  | NO2:89.1, O3:13.4 | 0.0546 | SO2:595.5, CO:0.39 | 0.02016 |
| 3  | PM10:230.4, PM2.5:133.9 | 0.0373 | NO2:878.7, CO:0.39 | 0.01959 |
| 4  | PM2.5:49.9, CO:1.18 | 0.0350 | PM10:3.9, PM2.5:3.31 | 0.01925 |
| 5  | PM2.5:133.9, PM10:230.4 | 0.0326 | PM2.5:4.77, PM10:5.7 | 0.01863 |
| 6  | PM10:158.6, PM2.5:133.9 | 0.0298 | PM2.5:3.31, PM10:3.9 | 0.01826 |
| 7  | CO:1.18, PM2.5:49.9 | 0.0283 | PM2.5:1.31, PM10:1.5 | 0.01764 |
| 8  | NO2:21.2, O3:88.0 | 0.0272 | NO2:913.2, CO:0.39 | 0.01739 |
| 9  | PM2.5:37.9, CO:0.99 | 0.0265 | PM2.5:7.09, PM10:8.5 | 0.01725 |
| 10 | PM2.5:133.9, PM10:158.6 | 0.0242 | PM10:2.7, PM2.5:2.25 | 0.01721 |

## 4.2   Research on Association Rules Mining Based on the Apriori Algorithm and ER Algorithm

**Time-Space Fusion Based on the ER Algorithm.** The ruleset of different months of the same monitoring station is time-integrated by the ER algorithm, wherein the weight of each ruleset is defined as domestic 0.2 and 0.143 abroad. Time fusion of data to obtain rulesets. And the rulesets is spatially fused by the ER method. In the process of spatial integration, the importance of monitoring stations is equal. In actual demand, some of the monitoring stations may be dominated by the rules, and the rest is used as a supplement and correction. In this case, the weight also needs to be changed accordingly, such as the geographical distance as a reference factor for weight determination. The results of the fusion of the top ten confidence ranking rules are shown in Table 8.

**Table 8.** The top ten rules of time-space fusion by the ER algorithms (China and USA)

|    | Rules (China)          | Confidence | Rules (China)           | Confidence |
|----|------------------------|------------|-------------------------|------------|
| 1  | O3:13.4, NO2:89.1      | 0.0435     | PM2.5:1.31, PM10:1.5    | 0.01370    |
| 2  | NO2:89.1, O3:13.4      | 0.0425     | PM10:1.5, PM2.5:1.31    | 0.01301    |
| 3  | PM2.5:49.9, CO:1.18    | 0.0317     | PM10:16.1, PM2.5:13.41  | 0.01188    |
| 4  | PM2.5:322.6, PM10:230.4| 0.0279     | PM2.5:13.41, PM10:16.1  | 0.01161    |
| 5  | NO2:21.2, O3:88.0      | 0.0271     | PM10:5.7, PM2.5:4.77    | 0.01053    |
| 6  | NO2:21.2, O3:180.1     | 0.0269     | PM2.5:4.7, PM10:5.7     | 0.01030    |
| 7  | PM10:230.4, PM2.5:133.9| 0.0268     | NO2:878.7, CO:0.39      | 0.01015    |
| 8  | CO:1.18, PM2.5:49.9    | 0.0254     | PM2.5:3.31, PM10:3.9    | 0.01000    |
| 9  | PM2.5:133.9, PM10:230.4| 0.0248     | PM2.5:7.09, PM10:8.5    | 0.00988    |
| 10 | PM2.5:25.5, O3:180.1   | 0.0241     | PM10:3.9, PM2.5:3.31    | 0.00980    |

**Space-Time Fusion Based on the ER Algorithm.** In the case that the ER algorithm has been able to handle high-conflict evidence, it is also to verify whether the space fusion framework in the model can make the model better after the time fusion. A comparative experiment of spatial first fusion and then time fusion was carried out. The top ten results of the final fusion are shown in Table 9.

After the first time fusion, then the spatial fusion and the first spatial fusion and then the time fusion are combined, the final result is obtained. In the final fusion result, although the rules are slightly different, the number of data items and the final rule are very small. Some pollutants are related to different data segments, it shows that the two pollutants are highly correlated.

**Table 9.** The top ten rules of space-time fusion by the ER algorithms (China and USA)

|    | Rules (China)          | Confidence | Rules (USA)             | Confidence |
|----|------------------------|------------|-------------------------|------------|
| 1  | NO2:21.2, O3:180.1     | 0.0678     | PM2.5:1.31, PM10:1.5    | 0.01373    |
| 2  | PM2.5:25.5, O3:180.1   | 0.0604     | PM10:1.5, PM2.5:1.31    | 0.01305    |
| 3  | O3:13.4, NO2:89.1      | 0.0420     | PM10:16.1, PM2.5:13.41  | 0.01166    |
| 4  | NO2:89.1, O3:13.4      | 0.0408     | PM2.5:13.41, PM10:16.1  | 0.01161    |
| 5  | O3:180.1, NO2:21.2     | 0.0396     | PM10:5.7, PM2.5:4.77    | 0.01053    |
| 6  | PM2.5:37.9, O3:180.1   | 0.0377     | PM2.5:4.77, PM10:5.7    | 0.01030    |
| 7  | PM10:230.4, PM2.5:133.9| 0.0370     | NO2:878.7, CO:0.39      | 0.01001    |
| 8  | NO2:21.2, O3:88.0      | 0.0364     | PM2.5:3.31, PM10:3.9    | 0.01000    |
| 9  | PM2.5:133.9, PM10:230.4| 0.0346     | PM2.5:7.09, PM10:8.5    | 0.00986    |
| 10 | O3:180.1, PM2.5:25.5   | 0.0321     | PM10:3.9, PM2.5:3.31    | 0.00981    |

## 5  Conclusion

A Association rule mining method based on the Apriori algorithm and D-S theory is proposed, which solves the problem of incomplete data mining from multiple monitoring stations. What's more, the final fusion results are interpretative, can draw practical and relevant information, and provide corresponding theoretical support for the prevention and control of air pollution problems.

A Association rule mining method based on the Apriori algorithm and the ER algorithm is proposed, which solves the problem of evidence conflict in special cases and the non-uniformity of importance from each fusion data set. The weight system is introduced into the model. By assigning different weights to the rulesets with different degrees of importance in the fusion process, the mining results that are more in line with the actual situation can be obtained, and the performance is better in the prediction. The results of this method are also interpretative, and the specific association rules obtained are applied in the prevention and control of air pollution, which can provide good theoretical and technical support.

**Acknowledgements.** The paper is supported by the National Key R&D Program of China (No. 2017YFF0108300).

## References

1. Karimipour, F., Kanani-Sadat, Y.: Mapping the vulnerability of asthmatic allergy prevalence based on environmental characteristics through fuzzy spatial association rule mining. J. Environ. Inf. **28**(1), 1–10 (2017)
2. Cagliero, L, Cerquitelli, T, Chiusano, S, et al.: Modeling correlations among air pollution-related data through generalized association rules. In: IEEE International Conference on Smart Computing, Kuala Lumpur, pp. 298–303 (2016)
3. Berrocal, V.J.: Space-time data fusion under error in computer model output: an application to modeling air quality. Biometrics **68**(3), 837–848 (2012)
4. Friberg, M.D., Chang, H.H., Kahn, R.A., et al.: Daily ambient air pollution metrics for five cities: evaluation of data fusion-based estimates and uncertainties. Atmos. Environ. **158**, 36–50 (2017)
5. Qian, Y., et al.: Research on multi-source data fusion in the field of atmospheric environmental monitoring. 13th International Conference on Computer Science & Education (ICCSE) (2018)
6. Liao, P.-C., Chen, H., Luo, X.: Fusion model for hazard association network development: a case in elevator installation and maintenance. KSCE J. Civ. Eng. **23**(4), 1451–1465 (2019). https://doi.org/10.1007/s12205-019-0646-5
7. Güder, M., Çiçekli, N.K.: Multi-modal video event recognition based on association rules and decision fusion. Multimedia Syst. **24**(1), 55–72 (2017). https://doi.org/10.1007/s00530-017-0535-z
8. Abdel-Basset, M., Mohamed, M., Smarandache, F., et al.: Neutrosophic association rule mining algorithm for big data analysis **10**, 106 (2018)
9. Zheng, H., Deng, Y.: Evaluation method based on fuzzy relations between Dempster-Shafer belief structure. Int. J. Intell. Syst. **33**(7), 1343–1363 (2018)
10. Deng, Y.: Generalized evidence theory. Appl. Intell. **43**(3), 530–543 (2015)

11. Florentin Smarandache, J.D.: Advences and Applications of DSmT for Information Fusion (Collected Works). American Research Press, Santa Fe (2006)
12. Murphy, C.K.: Combining belief functions when evidence conflicts. Decis. Support Syst. **29** (1), 1–9 (2000)
13. Du, Y., Wang, Y., Qin, M.: New evidential reasoning rule with both weight and reliability for evidence combination. Comput. Ind. Eng. **124**, 493–508 (2018)
14. Yang, J.B., Xu, D.L.: On the evidential reasoning algorithm for multiple attribute decision analysis under uncertainty. IEEE Trans. Syst. Man Cybern. Part A-Syst. Hum. **32**(3), 289–304 (2002)

# BLO: A Backtracking Based Layout Optimization Method for Time-Triggered Ethernet Topology Reconstruction

Yichen Wang[1], Qing Wang[2], Chenbang Wu[1]([✉]), Kuo Wang[2], Liping Teng[2], Wenjian Li[3], and Qinglong Han[4]

[1] Tianjin International Engineering Institute, Tianjin University, Tianjin, China
wuchenbang@tju.edu.cn
[2] School of Electrical and Information Engineering, Tianjin University, Tianjin, China
[3] Tianjin Jinhang Computing Technology Research Institute, Tianjin, China
[4] Beijing Institute of Spacecraft System Engineering, Beijing, China

**Abstract.** Time-Triggered Ethernet (TTE), as a novel communication architecture, highly requires for real-time data transmission and distributes widely in aerospace systems. However, the expensive cost of aircraft networks constrains the development of TTE to a large extent. Therefore, we are committed proposing an effective algorithm to optimize the complex networks and economize the physical cost while guaranteeing the real-time data transmission. At first, we generate the initial topology map according to the routing table given by the user. Subsequently, we adjust the number of switches and links respectively on the basis of our BLO algorithm, which unites backtracking algorithm and complex network theory. Furthermore, considering the convenience of our presentation, we design a topology reconstruction demo software. Finally, we demonstrate the reliability of our algorithm through experiments, and the result indicates that our algorithm is capable of optimizing the dual redundancy topological structure reasonably.

**Keywords:** Time-Triggered Ethernet · Topology reconstruction · BLO algorithm · Demo software

## 1 Introduction

For distributed avionics systems, the key to their system implementation is the real-time and deterministic communication between nodes. The real-time requirements of airborne networks have brought new demands and challenges to the design of avionics. Time-triggered Ethernet (TTE) has been widely used in aerospace industry with high real-time and high reliability. It combines the real-time, deterministic, and fault-tolerant of time-triggered technology with

Civil Areaspace Fundation No. [2016]1299.

W. Hong et al. (Eds.): NCCSTE 2019, CCIS 1216, pp. 99–112, 2020.
https://doi.org/10.1007/978-981-15-5390-5_9

the flexibility, dynamics, and "best effort" of traditional Ethernet to support synchronous, highly reliable embedded computer and network, fault-tolerant designs.

Kopetz et al. first proposed the concept of time-triggered Ethernet, which allows high-priority time-triggered messages to coexist with ordinary Ethernet event-triggered messages. The time-triggered protocol implemented by TTE on standard IEEE 802.3 Ethernet is fully compatible with the traditional Ethernet message transmission function and achieves contention-free time-triggered message transmission [1]. TTTech has modified the data link layer based on the standard Ethernet IEEE 802.3 protocol, and does not affect upper layer protocols such as UDP or IP [2].

The current topology reconstruction algorithm is mainly for software-defined networks or industrial Ethernet, with the aim of simplifying the network or improving network performance without considering the physical cost. The authors in [3] prove that having the set of network nodes it is possible to increase the network performance efficiency through wise management of routing information. The advantage of the proposed approach to routing management is its simple deployment both in current software-defined networks and across the separate set of independent communication channels that are united under the single controlling logic. The authors in [4] propose a novel resource preference aware routing algorithm. It can balance the network resources usage, decrease the amounts of resource bottlenecks and increase the acceptance rate of routing requests without introducing extra network load. The authors in [5] study the device allocation problem based on relative delay and real-time constraints, and simplifies the topology design problem of industrial Ethernet to the equipment allocation problem of industrial Ethernet, meeting the real-time diverse needs of industrial data streams.

At present, there are few studies on the topology of TTE networks. The authors in [6] propose an optimization method based on simulated annealing and designs a dual redundant TTE network topology. However, the deletion of the nodes in the process of constructing the topology is random, and the important nodes may be deleted, causing the message queue to be too long to cause congestion and affecting the reliability of the network.

This paper proposes a TTE network topology reconstruction method, which reconfigures the network connection situation for the given network structure and network delay requirements, continuously optimizes the network structure, and reduces the network physical cost while ensuring the network delay performance and security of important TT traffic. Finally, the optimized dual redundant network structure is given, and the redundant network topology reconstruction of TTE is completed.

## 2   TTE Network Model

Time-Triggered Ethernet is a new Ethernet communication technology that mixes time and event services. It can support different real-time and security-level message transmission requirements with mixed traffic transmission mode.

The transmitted traffic is divided into time-triggered (TT) traffic, rate-constraint (RC) traffic, and best-effort (BE) traffic according to time-critical characteristics. TT information has high real-time requirements, the highest priority, and its waiting time, delay, jitter, etc. are fixed. All TT information is sent on time according to the pre-designed schedule. The RC information needs to guarantee the maximum bandwidth interval and is sent in the free area where the TT information is sent. The BE information uses the remaining bandwidth of the network with the lowest priority [7].

For the mixed traffic in the TTE network, this paper uses the method of partition scheduling for traffic transmission [8]. The periodic scheduling table of the partition scheduling mode is shown in Fig. 1. The period length of the i-th TT tarffic is $period_i$, the minimum unit of the schedule is the Basic Period (BC), and the length $L_{BC}$ is the greatest common divisor of all TT tarffic periods:

$$L_{BC} = \gcd(period_i) \tag{1}$$

Several basic periods form a Matrix Cycle (MC), its length $L_{BC}$ is the least common multiple of all TT tarffic periods in the network:

$$L_{BC} = \text{lcm}(period_i) \tag{2}$$

Each BC is divided into two parts, the first part is used to send TT traffic, and the second part is used to send RC and BE traffic. From the vertical perspective, the periodic schedule is a parallel of n basic periods, which are connected end to end in sequence, and the total time of the n basic periods is the length of the matrix period. In the horizontal direction, each basic period consists of the TT frame of the first half and the RC+BE frame of the second half [9].

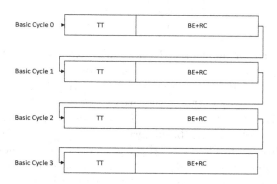

**Fig. 1.** Schematic diagram of periodic scheduling.

# 3    Optimization Objection

## 3.1    Delay Analysis of RC Traffic

In this paper, the transmission of TT and RC traffic adopts the timely blocking mode [10]. During the transmission of the RC traffic, as long as there is a TT traffic, the RC traffic transmission is terminated until the TT tarffic is transmitted and there is still an idle period to continue to send the RC tarffic. For a single RC tarffic, the bandwidth occupied by the transmission is the ratio of the maximum frame length to the maximum bandwidth interval of the RC information [11].

$$M_i = \frac{S_{RC_i,\max}}{BAG_{RC_i}} \tag{3}$$

where $M_i$ represents the maximum bandwidth that the RC stream can use on the virtual link, $S_{RC_i,\max}$ is the maximum frame length of the RC stream on the virtual link, and $BAG_{RC_i}$ is the maximum bandwidth allocation interval of the RC stream, in milliseconds.

The literature [12] proposes the use of deterministic network analysis to estimate the worst-case delay of RC streams in a TTE network. The delay of the RC stream at each node can be ascertained by using the maximum horizontal distance of the network's arrival curve and the service curve. In the network topology, the e1 end sends m RC streams, and the destination end is indefinite. The source end is limited by the maximum frame length and the minimum frame interval. Therefore, the worst delay of the m RC streams at the source end is [12]:

$$D_{RC_i}^0 = H(\alpha_{RC}^0, \beta_{RC}^0) = \left[ \frac{\sum\limits_{i=1}^{n} S_{RC_i,\max}}{C \left( l_{BC} - l_1 \right)} \right] l_{BC} + l_1 +$$

$$\left[ \frac{\sum\limits_{i=1}^{n} S_{RC_i,\max}}{C} - \left[ \frac{\sum\limits_{i=1}^{n} S_{RC_i,\max}}{C \left( l_{BC} - l_1 \right)} \right] \left( l_{BC} - l_1 \right) \right] \tag{4}$$

The arrival curve of the source RC stream is expressed as $\alpha_{RC}^0$, the service curve can be expressed as $\beta_{RC}^0$. $l_{BC}$ is the length of time in which the TT is located in the basic period. The maximum delay of the RC stream at each node is the horizontal distance between the arrival curve and the service curve at that node, C is the link's physical rate. In a time-triggered Ethernet, the TT schedule is designed offline. In a basic period, the time period configured by the TT stream is also fixed. Therefore, there is a worst case scenario. In a basic period, after sending all the TT streams to be sent, sending another RC stream will cause congestion. In this case, the delay in one basic period is [12]:

$$l_1 = l_{TT} + S_{RC,\max} \tag{5}$$

where $l_{TT}$ is the length of the TT stream sent in a basic period.

At the next node, if there are n RC streams, the arrival curve is expressed as $\alpha_{RC}^1$, and the service curve can be expressed as $\beta_{RC}^1$, $l_{BC}$ is the length of time in which the TT is occupied in the basic period. The delay of an RC stream at the next node is shown in Eq. (6).

$$D_{RC_i}^1 = H(\alpha_{RC}^1, \beta_{RC}^1) = \left[ \frac{\sum\limits_{i=1}^{n} S_{RC_i,\max} + \sum\limits_{i=1}^{n} \frac{S_{RC_i,\max}}{BAG_{RC_i}}}{C(l_{BC} - l_1)} \right] l_{BC} +$$

$$\left[ \frac{\sum\limits_{i=1}^{n} S_{RC_i,\max} + \sum\limits_{i=1}^{n} \frac{S_{RC_i,\max}}{BAG_{RC_i}} D_{RC_i}}{C} - \left[ \frac{\sum\limits_{i=1}^{n} S_{RC_i,\max} + \sum\limits_{i=1}^{n} \frac{S_{RC_i}}{BAG_{RC_i}} D_{RC_i}}{C(l_{BC} - l_1)} \right] (l_{BC} - l_1) \right]$$

$$(6)$$

The maximum delay that the $RC_i$ may generate at the output queue of the first node is $D_{RC_i}^1$. In the same way, the maximum delay $D_{RC_i}^2$, $D_{RC_i}^3$ ...$D_{RC_i}^n$ generated by the $RC_i$ in the queue of each node output can be obtained in turn. The delay of the RCI over the entire network link is the sum of the delays at each node:

$$D_{RC_i} = D_{RC_i}^0 + \sum_{j=1}^{k} D_{RC_i}^j \tag{7}$$

## 3.2   Physical Costs

The purpose of topology reconstruction of TTE network is to reduce the physical cost of the network by simplifying the network structure while ensuring the real-time and reliability of data transmission. Cost has always been an important limiting factor for the widespread use of the network, and reducing costs will bring greater flexibility and breadth to the deployment of the network. For a network topology, its physical cost consists of three parts: terminal, switch, and link. In the process of topology reconstruction, the terminal is fixed, so we mainly optimize the physical cost of the switch and link.

Here we use a physical cost function $cost(\Upsilon)$ to represent the total physical cost of switches and links in the network, where $\Upsilon$ denotes a network topology:

$$cost(\Upsilon) = N_s \cdot cost(switch) + N_L \cdot cost(link) \tag{8}$$

where $N_S$, $N_L$ are the number of switches and links in the network respectively. $cost(switch)$ and $cost(link)$ are the physical costs of a single switch and a single link that are artificially set.

As shown in Fig. 2, the topology $\Upsilon_0$, 6 terminals are connected by 3 switches and 11 links, then $N_s = 3$, $N_L = 11$. Suppose a switch has a physical cost of 20 and a link has a physical cost of 1. Then the physical cost of the topology is:

$$cost(\Upsilon_0) = 3 \times 20 + 11 \times 1 = 71 \tag{9}$$

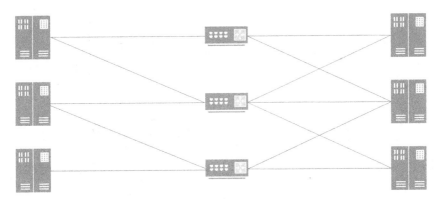

**Fig. 2.** The topology $\Upsilon_0$.

### 3.3   Objective Function

When the network structure is too simplified, a large number of RC tarffic will be crowded into a limited number of switches and several links, and the network will become very slow or even embarrassing.

In order to avoid this situation, we set an upper limit $RC_i deadline$ for each $RC_i$ tarffic, then compare the $D_{RC_i}$ and $RC_i deadline$ to determine whether the simplified network can smoothly transmission of all RC tarffic: if $D_{RC_i} - RC_i deadline \leq 0$, $RC_i$ delay does not exceed the upper limit, the reconstruction scheme is feasible; if $D_{RC_i} - RC_i deadline > 0$, $RC_i$ delay exceeds the upper limit, then the reconstruction plan needs to be combined with physical cost to determine whether it is feasible.

In order to find a balance between simplifying the network and guaranteeing RC on-time transmission, we introduce the optimization objective function $Object(\Upsilon)$ [6].

$$Object(\Upsilon) = cost(\Upsilon)+$$

$$\sum_{i=1}^{n} \begin{cases} \mu_1(D_{RC_i} - RC_i deadline)D_{RC_i} > RC_i deadline \\ \mu_2(D_{RC_i} - RC_i deadline)D_{RC_i} \leq RC_i deadline \end{cases} \quad (10)$$

$Object(\Upsilon)$ function is divided into two parts: physical cost and total topology delay. The physical cost is calculated by the $cost(\Upsilon)$ formula given in the previous section. The total topology delay is the weighted sum of the delays of all RC tarffic. Among them, $\mu_1$ and $\mu_2$ are the weights of the two delay states, where $\mu_1$ is a penalty weight which guarantees that the delay will not exceed the delay limit during the optimization process; and $\mu_2$ is a reward weight which represents the effect of the difference in delay on the objective function. When the delay in the network exceeds the upper limit, the optimization target value will also become infinite, and such a network will not be selected.

# 4   Betweenness Based Layout Optimization Algorithm BLO

The topology reconstruction of the TTE network introduces the delay analysis of the deterministic network, and combines the optimization strategy of the redundant network and the complex network theory. The goal is to simplify the network, and reduce the network cost as much as possible while ensuring the tarffic on-time transmission. At first, we convert the schedule given by the user into an adjacency matrix, and then generate an initial topology map. Subsequently, we considering to reducing the number of switches prior to the links, because the cost of switch is much higher. After that, we utilize the similar method to adjust the links. Furthermore, we design a dual redundant topology. The adjustment of the switch or the link may affect the transmission of the substream. When the normal transmission of the substream is affected, how to adjust the transmission path of the substream to ensure the performance of data transmission is the core problem to be solved. The TTE topology reconstruction flowchart is shown in Fig. 3.

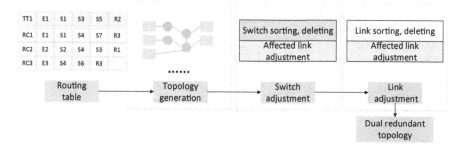

**Fig. 3.** TTE topology reconstruction flowchart

## 4.1   The Design of Switch Adjustment Module

The Switch adjustment strategy is presented in Fig. 4. Firstly, we confirm the choice strategies of the switches. We address the problem by introducing two definitions in the complex network theory, node-betweenness and edge-betweenness. The node-betweenness refers to the ratio of the number of paths passing through the node in the shortest path in the network to the total number of the shortest paths. And the edge-betweenness refers to the ratio of the number of paths through the link to the total number of the shortest paths among all the shortest paths in the network. We regard switches and links as nodes and links in complex network theory, respectively, sorting the importance of switches and links according to the node-betweenness and edge-betweenness, larger betweenness values mean greater importance, and deleting switches according to their importance from low to high. From practical considerations, we can't delete all the switches, and also consider the simplicity and rationality of the algorithm, we set an upper limit S to delete the switch. When the betweenness value of target switch is greater than S, we believe that the switch plays an important role in the system and will not be deleted. Secondly, we assume that deleting a switch and then calculating the optimization objective function. If the value of the optimization objective function is less than before, delete the switch, otherwise, return it. Thirdly, adjust the transmission path of the affected substreams. After a target switch is deleted, links connected to the switch are deleted. This may affect the normal transmission of some substreams. We filter the affected substreams, and find new paths to transmit them.

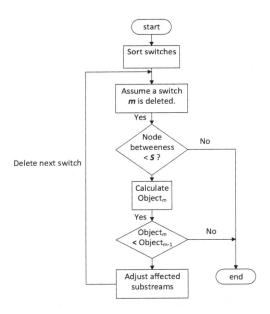

**Fig. 4.** The process of switch adjustment module

For how to adjust the transmission path of the affected substream, the steps are as shown in Fig. 5. The first step is to determine whether the currently existing device can transmit the affected sub-flow from the transmitting end to the receiving end after deleting the target switch and the link. If not, the new link needs to be added. The decision is based on backtracking algorithm. In the second step, the routing table is changed according to the current substream transmission path. In the third step, it is judged whether the substream link adjustment is completed. If not, the process returns to the first step, and if it is completed, the process ends.

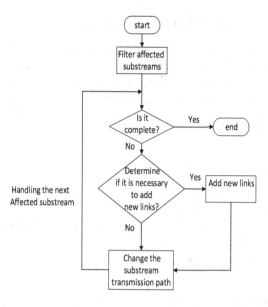

**Fig. 5.** The transmission path of the affected substream adjustment

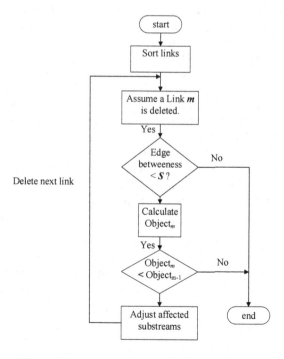

**Fig. 6.** The process of link adjustment module

## 4.2   The Design of Link Adjustment Module

It is similar to the switch adjustment module. Firstly, the links are sorted according to importance, and an upper bound value K is also set for the edge-betweeness. Secondly, we assume that a link is deleted, and determine whether the link should be deleted according to the optimization objective function. Thirdly, adjust the transmission path of the affected substream. The process of link adjustment module is shown in Fig. 6.

## 4.3   The Design of Dual Redundant Topology

Considering the need for aerospace systems to ensure high real-time and high reliability, we design the dual redundant topology. The Time-Triggered Ethernet combines real-time with non-real-time traffic, thus we aim to guarantee the real-time nature of TT traffic. We filter the switches and links that TT traffic involved, and make a copy of it as redundant topology.

# 5   Experimental Evaluation and Software Implementation

## 5.1   Experimental Evaluation

In order to verify the rationality of the topology reconstruction algorithm proposed in this paper, we take two sets of routing tables as an example. We use the algorithm proposed above to perform topology reconstruction, and analyze the comparison of various indicators.

The experimental comparison is shown as Table 1. NO. ESes, NO. Msgs represent the number of end system, data flow respectively. And NO. NSes, NO. links represent the number of switch, link respectively. For routing table line 1, after topology reconstruction, the number of switches has been reduced from 7 to 5, and the number of links has been reduced, from 15 to 10. The cost is cut down from 155 to 110. For routing table line 2, the number of NSes and links are all optimized, and the cost decreases by 43. The experimental result indicate that we appropriately reduce the cost of the architecture by utilizing the topology reconstruction algorithm we presented.

**Table 1.** The experimental comparison

| Table | NO.ESes | NO.Msgs | NO.NSes | | NO.links | | cost | |
|---|---|---|---|---|---|---|---|---|
| | | | Former | Latter | Former | Latter | Former | Latter |
| 1 | 6 | 8 | 7 | 5 | 15 | 10 | 155 | 110 |
| 2 | 5 | 11 | 7 | 5 | 15 | 13 | 156 | 113 |

## 5.2   Software Implementation

**Topology Reconstruction Software.** The topology reconstruction software is shown in Fig. 7. The interface consists of three parts:

(1) Add initial routing part: used to add the initial routing table, click the "ChooseFile - Initial route" button to add the TXT document of the routing information and generate an EXCEL table containing the initial routing matrix. Fig. 8 shows the added routing information. The meanings of the information are message's type and number, sender number, route switch number, and receiver number.

(2) Reconstruct Topology button: used to run the program to reconstruct the initial topology and generate an EXCEL file containing the reconstructed routing matrix.

(3) Topology display part: Click the "ChooseFile" button to select the initial routing matrix or the reconstructed routing matrix file. Click the "Topology display" button to display all terminals, switches and links at the top of the interface. The complete topology.

**Experimental Result.** Add the initial routing table as shown in Fig. 8, which contains 3 TT tarffic, 8 RC tarffic, 3 senders, 3 receivers, and 7 switches. The initial topology is shown in Fig. 9. If the physical cost of a switch is 20 and the physical cost of a link is 1, the physical cost of the network in the initial topology is:

$$cost(\Upsilon) = 7 \times 20 + 15 \times 1 = 155 \tag{11}$$

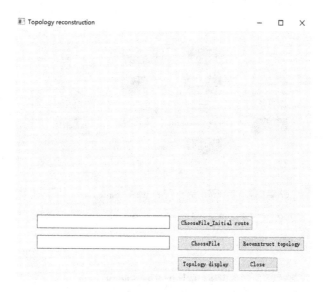

**Fig. 7.** Topology reconstruction software

The reconstructed topology is shown in Fig. 10. It contains 5 switches and 12 links, which is significantly simplified compared to the initial topology. The reconstructed network physical cost is:

$$cost(\Upsilon_f) = 5 \times 20 + 12 \times 1 = 112 \tag{12}$$

The physical cost after reconstruction is significantly reduced, which verifies the rationality and feasibility of the topology reconstruction algorithm and software.

tt1 E1 S1 S3 R1
tt2 E2 S2 S4 S3 R1
tt3 E3 S4 S7 S6 R3
rc1 E1 S1 S3 S5 R2
rc2 E1 S1 S2 S4 S7 S6 R3
rc3 E1 S1 S2 S4 S7 S6 S5 R2
rc4 E2 S2 S4 S3 R1
rc5 E2 S2 S4 S7 S3 S5 R2
rc6 E3 S4 S7 S5 R2
rc7 E3 S4 S3 R1
rc8 E3 S4 S6 R3

**Fig. 8.** Initial routing table

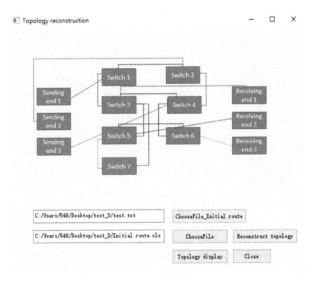

**Fig. 9.** Initial topology

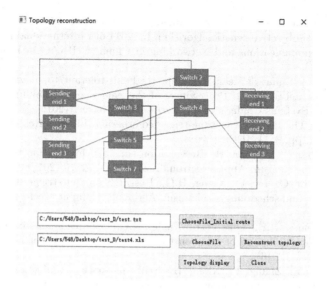

**Fig. 10.** Reconstructed topology

## 6 Conclusion

This paper introduces the related concepts of time-triggered Ethernet and proposes a topology reconstruction method for TTE networks. This method combines the delay analysis of the deterministic network and the optimization strategy of the redundant network. When the TT tarffic is transmitted on time and the RC tarffic is transmitted in time, the network is simplified and the physical cost of the network is reduced. The TTE topology reconstruction software is designed. The software has visual topology interface and topology reconstruction generation process. The proposed TTE topology reconstruction method is verified by examples, which proves the feasibility and rationality of the method and software.

## References

1. Steiner, W.: TTEthernet specification. TTTech Computertechnik AG, November 2008, 39–40 (2008)
2. SAE AS6802: Time-Triggered Ethernet. SAE International (2011)
3. Beshley, M., Seliuchenko, M., Panchenko, O., Polishuk, A.: Adaptive flow routing model in SDN. In: 2017 14th International Conference the Experience of Designing and Application of CAD Systems in Microelectronics (CADSM), pp. 298–302. IEEE (2017)
4. Lee, D., Hong, P., Li, J.: RPA-RA: A resource preference aware routing algorithm in software defined network. In: 2015 IEEE Global Communications Conference (GLOBECOM), pp. 1–6. IEEE (2015)

5. Zhang, L., Lampe, M., Wang, Z.: Topology design of industrial ethernet networks using a multi-objective genetic algorithm. In: 2011 6th International ICST Conference on Communications and Networking in China (CHINACOM), pp. 735–741. IEEE (2011)

6. Gavrilut, V., Tamas-Selicean, D., Pop, P.: Fault-tolerant topology selection for TTEthernet networks. In: Proceedings of the Safety and Reliability of Complex Engineered Systems Conference, pp. 4001–4009. Citeseer (2015)

7. Kopetz, H.: The rationale for time-triggered ethernet. In: 2008 Real-Time Systems Symposium, pp. 3–11. IEEE (2008)

8. Pan, Y., Zhang, Q., Quan, H.: Research on time synchronization technology and scheduling mechanism. Appl. Electron. Tech. **43**(1), 72–76 (2017)

9. Liu, W.C., Li, Q., He, F., Xiong, H.G.: Research on time-triggerd-ethernet synchronization and scheduling mechanism. Aeronaut. Comput. Tech. **41**(4), 122–127 (2011)

10. Ling, Y., Feng, H.E., Qiao, L.I., Xiong, H.G.: Modified holistic approach for worstcase latency bound of rate-constrained flow in TTEthernet networks. Comput. Eng. Des. (2016)

11. Dai, Z., He, F., Zhang, Y., Xiong, H.: Real-time path optimization algorithm of AFDX virtual link. Acta Aeronautica et Astronautica Sinica **6**, 21 (2015)

12. Zhao, L., Li, Q., Lin, W., Xiong, H.: Stochastic network calculus for analysis of latency on TTEthernet network. Acta Aeronautica ET Astronautica Sinica **37**(6), 1953–1962 (2016)

# Research on Maximizing User and Minimum Rate in Strong Interference WPCN with Downlink SWIPT

Taoshen Li[1,2(⊠)], Nan Xiao[2], and Zhe Wang[3]

[1] School of Information Engineering, Nanning University,
Nanning 530200, China
[2] School of Computer, Electronics and Information, Guangxi University,
Nanning 530004, China
tshli@gxu.edu.cn, xiaonanllc@gmail.com
[3] School of Information Science and Engineering,
Guangxi University for Nationalities, Nanning 530005, China
designbyyili@163.com

**Abstract.** The wireless powered communication networks (WPCN) is a new networking paradigm which only considers energy transmission in the downlink, no the need for information transmission. In many applications of WPCN, it is necessary to consider transmit information in the downlink. How to develop a transmission strategy to weigh the fairness and maximization of each user's uplink throughput is a research hotspot in WPCN. This paper proposed a new design scheme for joint transmission of energy and information in a strongly interfered multi-cell network. It combined simultaneous transmission of downlink wireless information and energy with WPCN to realize downlink energy transmission and two-way information transmission between base station and users. In this scheme, uplink power allocation, downlink time allocation and beamforming were used to maximize the minimum transmission rates of both uplink and downlink, so that made a tradeoff between performance and fairness of uplink and downlink information transmission for each user. Simulation results show that compared with the traditional transmission method, the proposed scheme significantly improves the minimum transmission rate of the users.

**Keywords:** Wireless powered communication networks · Simultaneous wireless information and power transfer · Power allocation · Time allocation · Beamforming

## 1 Introduction

Recently, radio frequency-based energy harvesting wireless networks (RF-EHWN) with energy constrained devices are investigated to improve network efficiency and stabilization [1]. At present, two technologies of the RF-EHWN have been generated based on the features of RF signals: simultaneous wireless information and power transfer (SWIPT) [2, 3] and wireless powered communication network (WPCN) [4–7].

© Springer Nature Singapore Pte Ltd. 2020
W. Hong et al. (Eds.): NCCSTE 2019, CCIS 1216, pp. 113–128, 2020.
https://doi.org/10.1007/978-981-15-5390-5_10

The SWIPT realizes the operation of wireless energy transfer (WET) and wireless information transfer (WIT) using the same waveform simultaneously, while the WPCN focuses on how the energy harvested by downlink can be used for uplink information transmission under the single-sender and multi-receiver network model. The sending strategy to balance the fairness and maximization of uplink throughput of each user is one of research topic in WPCN [3].

Most of the existing researches on WPCN are based on the capture-transmission protocol [8], which divides the communication process of a unit into two stages: downlink energy transmission and capture, uplink information transmission and decoding. The receiver first harvests the energy from the downlink transmission broadcast signal, then send independent uplink transmission information to the access point by using the harvested energy, and comprehensively optimizes the time allocation of the upper and lower rows to maximize the system throughput. The authors in [9] proposed a novel power allocation algorithm for multi-input multi-output (MIMO) downlink systems with simultaneous wireless information and power transfer (SIPT), which can completely suppress the multiuser interference and perform an outer-bound. In [10], optimal and sub-optimal time and power allocation schemes were proposed for the case of complete and incomplete self-interference elimination. [11] proposed a joint beamforming and resource allocation scheme to maximize the minimum capacity of WPCN and enable simultaneous uplink and downlink information transmission.

User collaboration is an effective way to improve the capacity, coverage and other performance of wireless communication systems. Therefore, user collaboration communication is introduced into the research of SWIPT and WPCN systems [12–14]. The authors in [15] studied user cooperation in the a two-user WPCN to achieve more balanced throughput optimization and proposed performance indicators to represent near and far user collaboration by jointly optimizing the time and power allocations. [16] considered the placement optimization of energy and information access points (APs) in WPCN, and proposed an alternating optimization method to minimizing the network deployment cost with minimum number of energy nodes (ENs) and access points(APs) by jointly optimize the locations of ENs and Aps. [17] presented a cooperative scheme among users in the WPCN and a new pricing strategy to motivate the use to actively participate in the collaborative process, which the strategy can reduced the expected costs to the uses and improve the reliability of user unlink communications.

The existing WPCN only considers energy transmission in downlink, but does not consider the requirement of information transmission. However, information needs to be transmitted bi-directionally in many application. For example, in sensor networks, operation instruction information is sent in the downlink. Considering energy balancing, interference and energy transmission requirements, this paper combines SWIPT with WPCN, and proposes a new design scheme for joint transmission of energy and information in a strongly interfered multi-cell network. This scheme divides the whole problem into two sub-problems: uplink and downlink, and maximizes the minimum downlink user transmission rate by solving the optimal uplink power allocation, downlink beamforming and time allocation, respectively. It can realize downlink energy transmission and two-way information transmission between base station and users, and improve the performance of energy transmission.

# 2 Network Model

## 2.1 Construction Ideas of Network Model

In the network model of single base station with multiple antennas and multi-user with single antenna, we apply SWIPT to the downlink of WPCN. In this model, the downlink RF signal used only for energy transmission carries the data information required by the user. The user who needs the data information decodes the received RF signal, and the user who does not need the data information captures the energy of the RF signal. In the uplink phase, the base station determines the energy demand of each user according to the collected ideal channel state information (CSI). In the downlink phase, on the premise of ensuring that the user can capture enough energy, the information transmission capacity of each user can be maximized by optimizing the time allocation ratio of energy and information transmission and the beamforming vector of the base station. A unit time is divided into several time slots by the time-switching method of SWIPT in the downlink phase, and each user can allocate several time slots in mutual exclusion to transmit information in turn. When a user transmits information in allocated time slot, all other users capture the energy of RF signal.

In this paper, we consider a cellular network for large-scale MIMO systems with strong inter-cell interference. There are $N$ cells in this network, and each cell has a base station with $M$ antennas and $K$ users with a single antenna. All users in each cell are divided into $F$ groups, and a time unit t is divided into two phases: up-link and down-link. In the downlink phase, the base station transmits the signal to the user by time switching (SWIPT), in which the same group of users has the same time allocation of energy capture and information decoding, each cell transmits at the same frequency, and has strong inter-cell interference; In the uplink phase, the user transmits the information to the base station, and the different frequencies are transmitted between cells without considering the inter cell interference.

It is assumed that the information transmitted by each user in the uplink phase includes the pilot tones used for uplink channel estimation, the information transmitted by the base station in the downlink phase includes the obtained complete CSI and the downlink channel estimation obtained according to the channel reciprocity, and each base station can share the CSI obtained with other base stations. In the downlink phase, multicarrier technology is used between users in the group, such as orthogonal frequency division multiplexing (OFDM). For the convenience of research, this paper simplifies the number of users in each group to one user, that is, $F = K$.

## 2.2 Channel Estimation

In the uplink phase, all users send pilot signals, and then each base station performs channel estimation. The uplink channel coefficient matrix between the base station in cell-$i$ and the user in cell-$j$ is $\mathbf{G}^{(i,j)} = \mathbf{H}^{(i,j)} (\mathbf{B}^{(i,j)})^{1/2}$. Where $\mathbf{G}^{(i,j)}$ is the $M \times K$ matrix,

$\left[\mathbf{G}^{(i,j)}\right]_{mk} = g_{mk}^{(i,j)}$ representing the uplink channel coefficient between the $m$-th antenna of the base station in cell-$i$ and user-$k$ in cell-$j$; $\mathbf{H}^{(i,j)}$ is the $M \times K$ matrix, $\left[\mathbf{H}^{(i,j)}\right]_{mk} = h_{mk}^{(i,j)} \sim \mathcal{CN}(0,1)$ representing the uplink independent Rayleigh fading coefficient between the $m$-th antenna of the base station in cell-$i$ and user-$k$ in cell-$j$, $\mathbf{B}^{(i,j)}$ is the $K \times K$ diagonal matrix, and the diagonal element $b_k^{(i,j)}$ represents the path loss of the channel between the base station in cell-$i$ and user-$k$ in cell-$j$. Because of $g_{mk}^{(i,j)} = h_{mk}^{(i,j)} \cdot \sqrt{b_k^{(i,j)}}$, there is $g_{mk}^{(i,j)} \sim \mathcal{CN}\left(0, b_k^{(i,j)}\right)$. It is assumed that the channel coefficient does not change in one time unit and changes in probability in the next time unit. According to the channel reciprocity, the downlink channel matrix is the conjugate transpose matrix of the uplink channel matrix, that is $(\mathbf{G}^{(i,j)})^H$. Where $\mathbf{g}_k^{(i,j)}$ is the $k$ column of the matrix, which represents the uplink channel coefficient vector between the base station in cell-$i$ and user-$k$ in cell-$j$.

## 2.3  Time Allocation Within a Cell

For each cell, according to the channel coefficient vector from each user in the cell to the base station of the cell, all users of the cell are divided into $F$ groups. The subgroup $f_k^{(j)}$ of user-$k$ in cell-$j$ and the channel coefficient vector $\mathbf{g}_k^{(j,j)}$ from the user-$k$ to the cell base station of the cell-$j$ satisfies the following mapping:

$$f_k^{(j)} = \begin{cases} 1, & \left\|\mathbf{g}_k^{(i,j)}\right\|_2 \in D_1^{(j)} \\ \vdots & \\ F, & \left\|\mathbf{g}_k^{(i,j)}\right\|_2 \in D_F^{(j)} \end{cases} \tag{1}$$

The information transmission time of user-$k$ in cell-$j$ in the downlink phase and its subgroup meets the following mapping:

$$t_k^{(j)} = \begin{cases} \tau_1^{(j)} T, f_k^{(j)} = 1 \\ \vdots \\ \tau_F^{(j)} T, f_k^{(j)} = F \end{cases} \tag{2}$$

Where, $\sum\limits_{f=1}^{K} \tau_f^{(j)} = 1$.

Figure 1 shows the time allocation in the up and down phases, Where $T$ is the total time of the downlink phase and $\tau^{UL}$ the time of the uplink phase. In the downlink phase, the $f_k^{(j)}$-th user decodes the received RF signal in the allocated time $t_k^{(j)}$, and captures the energy in the rest time. Assume that the downlink time allocation vector in cell-$j$ is $\mathbf{t}^{(j)} = \begin{bmatrix} t_1^{(j)} & t_2^{(j)} & \cdots & t_K^{(j)} \end{bmatrix}^T$. In practical application, because the division of time is discrete, that is, a unit time can only be divided into finite equal parts, so the value range of $t_k^{(j)}$ is actually a finite discrete value, and the value space of $\mathbf{t}^{(j)}$ is a set of finite discrete vectors, which is denoted by $\mathbf{t}^{(j)} \in \mathbf{T}^{K \times 1}$.

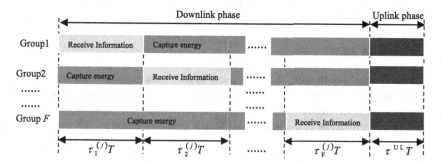

**Fig. 1.** Time allocation in the uplink and downlink phases

## 2.4    Downlink Phase

The baseband signal with information received by user-$k$ in cell-$j$ is

$$y_k^{(j)} = \sum_{i=1}^{N} \left( \mathbf{g}_k^{(i,j)} \right)^H \mathbf{w}^{(i)} \sqrt{q^{(i)}} s^{\mathrm{DL}(i)} + n_k^{(j)} \tag{3}$$

Where, $q^{(i)}$ is the transmission power of the base station of the cell-$i$ in the downlink phase, $\mathbf{w}^{(i)}$ is the beamforming vector ($M \times 1$) of the base station in cell-$i$, $\left\| \mathbf{w}^{(i)} \right\|_2 = 1$; $s^{\mathrm{DL}(i)} \sim \mathcal{CN}(0,1)$ is the information transmitted by the base station in cell-$i$, $n_k^{(j)} \sim \mathcal{CN}(0, \sigma^2)$ is the environmental noise of user-$k$ in cell-$j$ and assuming that the noise cannot be captured.

The energy captured by user-$k$ in cell-$j$ is

$$e_k^{(j)} = \left( 1 - t_k^{(j)} \right) \eta_k^{(j)} \cdot \sum_{i=1}^{N} \left| \sqrt{q^{(i)}} \left( \mathbf{g}_k^{(i,j)} \right)^H \mathbf{w}^{(i)} \right|^2 \tag{4}$$

Where the $\eta_k^{(j)} (0 < \eta_k^{(j)} \leq 1)$ is the energy capture efficiency.

Considering the estimation error, the baseband signal with information received by user-$k$ in cell-$j$ is

$$y_k^{(j)} = \left( \mathbf{g}_k^{(j,j)} \right)^H \mathbf{w}^{(j)} \sqrt{q^{(i)}} s^{\mathrm{DL}(j)} + \sum_{i=1,i \neq j}^{N} \left( \mathbf{g}_k^{(i,j)} \right)^H \mathbf{w}^{(i)} \sqrt{q^{(i)}} s^{\mathrm{DL}(i)} + n_k^{(j)} \tag{5}$$

The downlink information transmission rate of user-$k$ in cell-$j$ is

$$R_k^{\mathrm{DL}(j)} = t_k^{(j)} \cdot \log_2 \left( \frac{\sum_{i=1}^{N} q^{(i)} \left| \left( \mathbf{g}_k^{(i,j)} \right)^H \mathbf{w}^{(i)} \right|^2 + \sigma^2}{\sum_{i=1, i \neq j}^{N} q^{(i)} \left| \left( \mathbf{g}_k^{(i,j)} \right)^H \mathbf{w}^{(i)} \right|^2 + \sigma^2} \right) \tag{6}$$

### 2.5  Uplink Phase

Within the time $\tau^{\mathrm{UL}}$ of the uplink phase, users in each cell can simultaneously carry on uplink transmission to the cell base station. If the cross cell mobility of users is not considered, the interference between cells can be avoided by cross frequency transmission of users between cells, and the baseband signal received by the base station in cell-$j$ is

$$\mathbf{z}^{(j)} = \mathbf{G}^{(j,j)} \mathbf{x}^{(j)} + \mathbf{n}^{(j)} \tag{7}$$

Where, $\mathbf{x}^{(j)} = \left[ \sqrt{p_1^{(j)}} \cdot s_1^{\mathrm{UL}(j)} \quad \sqrt{p_2^{(j)}} \cdot s_2^{\mathrm{UL}(j)} \quad \cdots \quad \sqrt{p_K^{(j)}} \cdot s_K^{\mathrm{UL}(j)} \right]^T$, $p_k^{(j)}$ is the transmit power of user-k in cell-j in the downlink phase, $s_k^{UL(j)} \sim \mathcal{CN}(0,1)$ is the independent information uploaded to the base station by user-$k$ in cell-$j$, and $\mathbf{n}^{(j)} \sim \mathcal{CN}(0_{M \times 1}, \sigma^2 \cdot 1_{M \times 1})$ is the environmental noise vector. For the base station in the uplink phase, each user can send information at the same time, so the linear detection algorithm with lower complexity can be used for detection. The signal detected by linear detector $\mathbf{A}^{(j)}$ is $\mathbf{r}^{(j)} = \left( \mathbf{A}^{(j)} \right)^H \mathbf{G}^{(j,j)} \mathbf{X}^{(j)} + \left( \mathbf{A}^{(j)} \right)^H \mathbf{n}^{(j)}$. Typical linear detection algorithms are as follows:

(1)  Maximum ratio combining (MRC):

$$\mathbf{A}^{(j)} = \mathbf{G}^{(j,j)} \tag{8}$$

(2)  Zero Forcing (ZF):

$$\mathbf{A}^{(j)} = \mathbf{G}^{(j,j)} \left( \left( \mathbf{G}^{(j,j)} \right)^H \mathbf{G}^{(j,j)} \right)^{-1} \tag{9}$$

(3)  Minimum mean square error (MMSE) [18]:

$$\mathbf{A}^{(j)} = \mathbf{G}^{(j,j)} \left( \left( \mathbf{G}^{(j,j)} \right)^H \mathbf{G}^{(j,j)} + \frac{1}{p^{\mathrm{UL}}} \mathbf{I}_{k \times k} \right)^{-1} \tag{10}$$

Where, the $p^{UL}$ in MMSE algorithm is the unified transmission power of each user in the uplink phase. In this paper, because the transmission power of each user in the uplink phase is different, MMSE detector needs to be derived again.

For user transmit power matrix $\mathbf{P}^{(j)} = \mathrm{diag}\left\{ p_1^{(j)} \quad p_2^{(j)} \quad \cdots \quad p_K^{(j)} \right\}$ in cell-$j$, the detector of the MMSE is

$$\mathbf{A}^{(j)} = \left( \mathbf{G}^{(j,j)} \mathbf{P}^{(j)} \left( \mathbf{G}^{(j,j)} \right)^H + \sigma^2 \mathbf{I}_{M \times M} \right)^{-1} \mathbf{G}^{(j,j)} \mathbf{P}^{(j)} \tag{11}$$

The signal of user-$k$ in cell-$j$ detected by the base station in cell-$j$ by linear detector $\mathbf{A}^{(j)}$ is

$$r_k^{(j)} = \left( \mathbf{a}_k^{(j)} \right)^H \mathbf{g}_k^{(j,j)} \sqrt{p_k^{(j)}} s_k^{(j)} + \left( \mathbf{a}_k^{(j)} \right)^H \sum_{l=1,l\neq k}^{K} \mathbf{g}_l^{(j,j)} \sqrt{p_l^{(j)}} s_l^{UL(j)} + \left( \mathbf{a}_k^{(j)} \right)^H \mathbf{n}^{(j)} \tag{12}$$

Where, $\mathbf{a}_k^{(j)}$ is the $k$ column of matrix $\mathbf{A}^{(j)}$.

Therefore, in the uplink phase, the signal to interference plus noise (SINR) of user-$k$ in the cell received by the base station in cell-$j$ through the detector $\mathbf{A}^{(j)}$ is

$$\mathrm{SINR}_k^{UL(j)} = \frac{\left| \left( \mathbf{a}_k^{(j)} \right)^H \mathbf{g}_k^{(j,j)} \right|^2 p_k^{(j)}}{\sum_{l=1,l\neq k}^{K} \left| \left( \mathbf{a}_k^{(j)} \right)^H \mathbf{g}_l^{(j,j)} \right|^2 p_l^{(j)} + \left\| \mathbf{a}_k^{(j)} \right\|_2^2 \sigma^2} \tag{13}$$

According to Shannon formula, the uplink transmission rate of user-$k$ in cell-$j$ is

$$R_k^{UL(j)} = \tau^{UL} \cdot \log_2 \left( \frac{\sum_{l=1}^{K} \left| \left( \mathbf{a}_k^{(j)} \right)^H \mathbf{g}_l^{(j,j)} \right|^2 p_l^{(j)} + \left\| \mathbf{a}_k^{(j)} \right\|_2^2 \sigma^2}{\sum_{l=1,l\neq k}^{K} \left| \left( \mathbf{a}_k^{(j)} \right)^H \mathbf{g}_l^{(j,j)} \right|^2 p_l^{(j)} + \left\| \mathbf{a}_k^{(j)} \right\|_2^2 \sigma^2} \right) \tag{14}$$

## 3  Solution of Problem

The problem can be divided into two parts: uplink phase and downlink phase. In the uplink phase, the uplink transmission power of each user in each cell is solved by maximizing the minimum rate, and the soled result is input to the downlink phase as a parameter. In the downlink phase, the beamforming vector of the base station in each cell and the time allocation vector of energy acquisition and information decoding of each user group are also solved by maximizing the minimum rate. The optimization methods of the two stages are described as follows.

### 3.1 Uplink Phase Optimization

In the uplink phase, because the cross frequency transmission between cells does not interfere with each other, the $j$ ($j = 1,2,...,N$) cells can be described as $N$ independent problems. Therefore, the minimum uplink transmission rate $R_k^{\text{UL}(j)}$ of all users in cell-$j$ can be maximized to:

$$
\mathcal{P}_{\text{UL1}}^{(j)} : \underset{p_k^{(j)}}{\text{maximize}} \ \underset{1 \le k \le k}{\min} \left\{ R_k^{\text{UL}(j)} \right\} \tag{15}
$$

$$
\text{s.t} \quad p_k^{(j)} \le p_k^{\text{max}(j)}, \ \forall k \in \{1, 2, \ldots, K\}
$$

For a given $\tau^{\text{UL}}$, since $R_k^{\text{UL}(j)} = \tau^{\text{UL}} \cdot \log_2 \left( 1 + \text{SINR}_k^{\text{UL}(j)} \right)$ is a monotonic increasing function, the intermediate variable $\theta$ is introduced, and the optimization problem can be transformed as following

$$
\mathcal{P}_{\text{UL 2}}^{(j)} : \underset{\mathbf{P}^{(j)}, \theta}{\text{maximize}} \ \theta
$$

$$
\text{s.t.} \quad \theta \le \text{SINR}_k^{\text{UL}(j)}, \forall k \in \{1, 2, \ldots, K\} \tag{16}
$$

$$
\mathbf{P}^{(j)} \preccurlyeq \mathbf{P}^{\text{max}(j)}
$$

Where, $\mathbf{p}^{(j)} = \left[ p_1^{(j)} \ p_2^{(j)} \cdots p_k^{(j)} \right]$, $\mathbf{p}^{\text{max}(j)} = \left[ p_1^{\text{max}(j)} \ p_2^{\text{max}(j)} \cdots p_k^{\text{max}(j)} \right]^T$, $p_k^{\text{max}(j)}$ is the uplink maximum power of user-$k$ in cell-$j$. For the ZF, MRC and MMSE, $\text{SINR}_k^{\text{UL}(j)}$ has three corresponding expressions. The problems $\mathcal{P}_{\text{UL1}}^{(j)}$ can be transformed into $\mathcal{P}_{\text{UL}-\text{ZF}}^{(j)}$, $\mathcal{P}_{\text{UL}-\text{MRC}}^{(j)}$, and $\mathcal{P}_{\text{UL}-\text{MMSE}}^{(j)}$ respectively. They are expressed as follows

$$
\mathcal{P}_{\text{UL}-\text{ZF}}^{(j)} : \underset{\mathbf{P}^{(j)}, \theta}{\text{maximize}} \ \theta
$$

$$
\text{s.t.} \quad \theta \le \frac{1}{\left[ \left( \left( \mathbf{G}^{(jj)} \right)^H \mathbf{G}^{(jj)} \right)^{-1} \right]_{kk}} \cdot \frac{p_k^{(j)}}{\sigma^2}, \forall k \in \{1, 2, \ldots, K\} \tag{17}
$$

$$
\mathbf{P}^{(j)} \preccurlyeq \mathbf{p}^{\text{max}(j)}
$$

$$
\mathcal{P}_{\text{UL}-\text{MRC}}^{(j)} : \underset{\mathbf{P}^{(j)}, \theta}{\text{maximize}} \ \theta
$$

$$
\text{s.t.} \quad \theta \le \frac{\left\| \mathbf{g}_k^{(j,j)} \right\|_2^2 p_k^{(j)}}{\sum_{l=1, l \ne k}^{k} \frac{\left| \left( \mathbf{g}_k^{(jj)} \right)^H \mathbf{g}_k^{(jj)} \right|^2}{\left\| \mathbf{g}_k^{(jj)} \right\|_2^2} p_l^{(j)} + \sigma^2}, \forall k \in \{1, 2, \ldots K\} \tag{18}
$$

$$
\mathbf{p}^{(j)} \preccurlyeq \mathbf{p}^{\text{max}(j)}
$$

$$\mathcal{P}_{\text{UL--MMSE}}^{(j)} : \underset{\mathbf{p}^{(j)},\theta}{\text{maximize}}\ \theta$$

$$\text{s.t.}\quad \frac{\sigma^2 \theta}{1+\theta} \le \left(\mathbf{g}_k^{(j,j)}\right)^H \mathbf{g}_k^{(j,j)} - \frac{\sum\limits_{l=1}^{K} p_l^{(j)} \left(\mathbf{g}_k^{(j,j)}\right) \mathbf{g}_k^{(j,j)} \left(\mathbf{g}_k^{(j,j)}\right)^H \left(\mathbf{g}_k^{(j,j)}\right)}{\sigma^2 + \text{tr}\left(\sum\limits_{l=1}^{K} p_l^{(j)} \mathbf{g}_l^{(j,j)} \left(\mathbf{g}_l^{(j,j)}\right)^H\right)}, \tag{19}$$

$$\forall k \in \{1, 2, \ldots, K\}$$

$$\mathbf{p}^{(j)} \preccurlyeq \mathbf{p}^{\text{max}(j)}$$

## 3.2 Downlink Phase Optimization

In the downlink phase, the multi-objective optimization problem of the downlink transmission rate of user-$k$ ($1 \le k \le K$) in each cell can be transformed into a single objective optimization problem by minimizing and maximizing the optimization method again. The optimized formula is

$$\mathcal{P}_{\text{DL1}} : \underset{\mathbf{w}^{(j)},\mathbf{t}^{(j)}}{\text{maximize}}\ \underset{1 \le j \le N}{\text{min}} \left\{ \underset{1 \le k \le K}{\text{min}} \left\{ R_k^{\text{DL}(j)} \right\} \right\}$$

$$\text{s.t.}\quad e_k^{(j)} \le \tau^{\text{UL}} p_k^{(j)}, \forall j \in \{1, 2, \ldots, N\}, \forall k \in \{1, 2, \ldots, K\} \tag{20}$$

$$\mathbf{t}^{(j)} \in \mathbf{T}^{K \times 1}$$

$$\left\| \mathbf{w}^{(j)} \right\|_2 = 1$$

Where, $R_l^{\text{DL}(j)} = t_k^{(j)} \cdot \log_2 \left( 1 + \dfrac{q^{(j)} \left| \left(\mathbf{g}_k^{(j,j)}\right)^H \mathbf{w}^{(j)} \right|^2}{\sum\limits_{i=1,i \ne j}^{N} q^{(i)} \left| \left(\mathbf{g}_k^{(j,j)}\right)^H \mathbf{w}^{(j)} \right|^2 + \sigma^2} \right)$,

$$e_k^{(j)} = \left( 1 - t_k^{(j)} \right) \eta_k^{(j)} \cdot \sum_{i=1}^{N} \left| \sqrt{q^{(i)}} \left(\mathbf{g}_k^{(i,j)}\right)^H \mathbf{w}^{(i)} \right|^2 \tag{21}$$

For a given $\mathbf{t}^{(j)} = \begin{bmatrix} t_1^{(j)} & t_2^{(j)} & \cdots & t_K^{(j)} \end{bmatrix}^T$, the solution of $\mathcal{P}_{\text{DL1}}$ can be transformed into the solution of $\mathcal{P}_{\text{DL2}}\left(\mathbf{t}^{(j)}\right)$ which removes the constraint $\mathbf{t}^{(j)} \in \mathbf{T}^{K \times 1}$, and then traverses $\mathbf{t}^{(j)} \in \mathbf{T}^{K \times 1}$ and finds out the value of the $\mathbf{t}^{(j)}$ which solves $\mathcal{P}_{\text{DL2}}\left(\mathbf{t}^{(j)}\right)$.

We define the augmented matrix $\tilde{\mathbf{w}} = \begin{bmatrix} \left(\mathbf{w}^{(1)}\right)^T & \left(\mathbf{w}^{(2)}\right)^T & \cdots & \left(\mathbf{w}^{(N)}\right)^T \end{bmatrix}^T$, then there is $\mathbf{w}^{(j)} = \mathbf{E}^{(j)} \tilde{\mathbf{w}}$. Where, $\mathbf{E}^{(j)}$ is the $M \times (N \cdot M)$ matrix with $M \times M$ unit matrix from column $(j-1)M+1$ to column $jM$ and all other elements are zero. The Definitions of $\mathbf{A}_k^{(j)}, \mathbf{B}_k^{(j)}, \mathbf{C}_k^{(j)}$ and $\mathbf{E}^{(j)}$ are as follows

$$\mathbf{A}_k^{(j)} = q^{(j)} \left(\mathbf{E}^{(j)}\right)^H \mathbf{g}_k^{(j,j)} \left(\mathbf{g}_k^{(j,j)}\right)^H \mathbf{E}^{(j)} \tag{22}$$

$$\mathbf{B}_k^{(j)} = \sum_{i=1,i\neq j}^{N} q^{(i)} \left(\mathbf{E}^{(i)}\right)^H \mathbf{g}_k^{(i,j)} \left(\mathbf{g}_k^{(i,j)}\right)^H \mathbf{E}^{(i)} + \sigma^2 \left(\mathbf{E}^{(j)}\right)^H \mathbf{E}^{(j)} \tag{23}$$

$$\mathbf{C}_k^{(j)} = \eta_k^{(j)} \cdot \sum_{i=1}^{N} q^{(i)} \left(\mathbf{E}^{(i)}\right)^H \mathbf{g}_k^{(i,j)} \left(\mathbf{g}_k^{(i,j)}\right)^H \mathbf{E}^{(i)} \tag{24}$$

$$\mathbf{D}^{(j)} = \left(\mathbf{E}^{(i)}\right)^H \mathbf{E}^{(i)} \tag{25}$$

Then:

$$R_k^{\mathrm{DL}(j)} = t_k^{(j)} \cdot \log_2 \left(1 + \frac{\tilde{\mathbf{w}}^H \mathbf{A}_k^{(j)} \tilde{\mathbf{w}}}{\tilde{\mathbf{w}}^H \mathbf{B}_k^{(j)} \tilde{\mathbf{w}}}\right) \tag{26}$$

$$e_k^{(j)} = \left(1 - t_k^{(j)}\right) \tilde{\mathbf{w}}^H \mathbf{C}_k^{(j)} \tilde{\mathbf{w}} \tag{27}$$

$\mathcal{P}_{\mathrm{DL2}}\left(\mathbf{t}^{(j)}\right)$ can be expressed as follows

$$\mathcal{P}_{\mathrm{DL2}}\left(\mathbf{t}^{(j)}\right) : \underset{\tilde{\mathbf{w}}}{\text{maximize}} \min_{1 \leq j \leq N, 1 \leq k \leq K} \left\{ t_k^{(j)} \cdot \log_2 \left(1 + \frac{\tilde{\mathbf{w}}^H \mathbf{A}_k^{(j)} \tilde{\mathbf{w}}}{\tilde{\mathbf{w}}^H \mathbf{B}_k^{(j)} \tilde{\mathbf{w}}}\right) \right\}$$

$$\text{s.t.} \qquad \tilde{\mathbf{w}}^H \mathbf{C}_k^{(j)} \tilde{\mathbf{w}} \geq \frac{\tau^{\mathrm{UL}} p_k^{(j)}}{1 - t_k^{(j)}}, \forall j \in \{1, 2, \ldots, N\}, \forall k \in \{1, 2, \ldots, K\}$$

$$\tilde{\mathbf{w}}^H \left(\mathbf{E}^{(j)}\right)^H \mathbf{E}^{(j)} \tilde{\mathbf{w}} = 1, \forall j \in \{1, 2, \ldots, N\} \tag{28}$$

We introduce the intermediate variable $\theta$, and the optimization formula can be expressed as follows

$$\mathcal{P}_{\mathrm{DL3}}\left(\mathbf{t}^{(j)}\right) : \underset{\tilde{\mathbf{w}}, \theta}{\text{maximize}} \; \theta$$

$$\text{s.t.} \qquad \tilde{\mathbf{w}}^H \mathbf{A}_k^{(j)} \tilde{\mathbf{w}} \geq \left(2^{\frac{\theta}{t_k^{(j)}}} - 1\right) \tilde{\mathbf{w}}^H \mathbf{B}_k^{(j)} \tilde{\mathbf{w}}, \forall j \in \{1, 2, \ldots, N\}, \forall k \in \{1, 2, \ldots, K\}$$

$$\tilde{\mathbf{w}}^H \mathbf{C}_k^{(j)} \tilde{\mathbf{w}} \geq \frac{\tau^{\mathrm{UL}} p_k^{(j)}}{1 - t_k^{(j)}}, \forall j \in \{1, 2, \ldots, N\}, \forall k \in \{1, 2, \ldots, K\}$$

$$\tilde{\mathbf{w}}^H \mathbf{D}^{(j)} \tilde{\mathbf{w}} = 1, \forall j \in \{1, 2, \ldots, N\} \tag{29}$$

The rank-1 matrix W of $(N \cdot M) \times (N \cdot M)$ is defined as: $\mathbf{W} = \tilde{\mathbf{W}}\tilde{\mathbf{W}}^H$. For the given intermediate variable $\theta$ and $\mathbf{t}^{(j)}$, Optimization problems can be transformed into

$\mathcal{P}_{DL4}\left(\theta, \mathbf{t}^{(j)}\right)$ : Find $\mathbf{W}$

s.t. $\quad \mathrm{tr}\left(\left(2^{\frac{\theta}{t_k^{(j)}}} - 1\right)\mathbf{B}_k^{(j)}\mathbf{W}\right) \geq 0, \forall j \in \{1, 2, \ldots, N\}, \forall k \in \{1, 2, \ldots, K\}$

$\mathrm{tr}\left(\left(\mathbf{A}_k^{(j)} - \left(2^{\frac{\theta}{t_k^{(j)}}} - 1\right)\mathbf{B}_k^{(j)}\right)\mathbf{W}\right) \geq 0, \forall j \in \{1, 2, \ldots, N\}, \forall k \in \{1, 2, \ldots, K\}$

$\mathrm{tr}\left(\mathbf{C}_k^{(j)}\mathbf{W}\right) \geq \frac{\tau^{UL}p_k^{(j)}}{1-t_k^{(j)}}, \forall j \in \{1, 2, \ldots, N\}, \forall k \in \{1, 2, \ldots, K\}$

$\mathrm{tr}\left(\mathbf{D}^{(j)}\mathbf{W}\right) = 1, \forall j \in \{1, 2, \ldots, N\}$

$\mathbf{W} \succcurlyeq \mathbf{0}$

$\mathrm{rank}(\mathbf{W}) = 1$

$$(30)$$

If the constraint $\mathrm{rank}(\mathbf{W}) = 1$ is ignored, the solution $\mathbf{W}^*$ can be obtained by semidefinite relaxation method [19]. Generally, $\mathbf{W}^*$ is a full rank matrix and does not satisfy the constraint $\mathrm{rank}(\mathbf{W}) = 1$. The approximate rank one matrix $\mathbf{W}_1^* 1$ of $\mathbf{W}^*$ can be taken as the approximate solution of $\mathcal{P}_{DL4}\left(\theta, \mathbf{t}^{(j)}\right)$. Set $\mathrm{rank}(\mathbf{W}^*) = r$, its eigenvalue is $\lambda_1 \geq \lambda_2 \geq \ldots \geq \lambda_r > 0$, and the corresponding eigenvector is $\mathbf{u}_1, \mathbf{u}_2, \ldots, \mathbf{u}_r$, then $\mathbf{W}^* = \sum_{i=1}^{r} \lambda_i \mathbf{u}_i \mathbf{u}_i^H$. Because the coefficient matrices $\mathbf{A}_k^{(j)}, \mathbf{B}_k^{(j)}, \mathbf{C}_k^{(j)}$ are sparse matrices, $\mathbf{W}^*$ is also sparse matrix, and meets the following requirements:

$$\mathbf{W}^* = \begin{bmatrix} \mathbf{W}^{(1)*} & \mathbf{0} & \cdots & \mathbf{0} \\ \mathbf{0} & \mathbf{W}^{(2)*} & \cdots & \mathbf{0} \\ \vdots & \vdots & \ddots & \vdots \\ \mathbf{0} & \mathbf{0} & \cdots & \mathbf{W}^{(N)*} \end{bmatrix} \qquad (31)$$

Where, $\mathbf{W}^{(j)*} = \mathbf{E}^{(j)*}\mathbf{W}^*(\mathbf{E}^{(j)})^H (j = 1, 2, \ldots, N)$. For $\mathbf{W}^{(j)*}$, its eigenvalue is $\lambda_1^{(j)} \geq \lambda_2^{(j)} \geq \ldots \geq \lambda_{r^{(j)}}^{(j)} > 0$ and the corresponding eigenvector is $\mathbf{u}_1^{(j)}, \mathbf{u}_2^{(j)}, \ldots, \mathbf{u}_{r^{(j)}}^{(j)}$. The approximate rank-1 matrices $\mathbf{W}_1^{(j)*}$ can be expressed as $\mathbf{W}_1^{(j)*} = \lambda_1^{(j)}\mathbf{u}_1^{(j)}\left(\mathbf{u}_1^{(j)}\right)^H$. Therefore, the approximate solution of the beamforming vector of the base station in cell-$j$ is $\mathbf{w}^{(j)*} = \sqrt{\lambda_1^{(j)}}_1 \mathbf{u}_1^{(j)}$, that is, the approximate solution of the $\mathcal{P}_{DL4}\left(\theta, \mathbf{t}^{(j)}\right)$.

For user-$k$ in cell-$j$, according to the optimal solution $p_k^{(j)*}$ of its uplink transmission phase, the time allocation ratio $\tau_k^{(j)}$ and power split ratio $\gamma_k^{(j)}$ of its downlink transmission satisfy the following requirements:

$$\left(1-\tau_k^{(j)}\right)\eta_k^{(j)} \cdot \sum_{i=1}^{N}\left|\sqrt{q^{(i)}}\left(\mathbf{g}_k^{(i,j)}\right)^H \mathbf{w}^{(i)*}\right|^2 = \tau^{\mathrm{UL}}p_k^{(j)*} \qquad (32)$$

$$\left(1-\gamma_k^{(j)}\right)\eta_k^{(j)} \cdot \sum_{i=1}^{N}\left|\sqrt{q^{(i)}}\left(\mathbf{g}_k^{(i,j)}\right)^H \mathbf{w}^{(i)*}\right|^2 = \tau^{\mathrm{UL}}p_k^{(j)*} \qquad (33)$$

Therefore, the optimal solution of $\tau_k^{(j)}$ and $\gamma_k^{(j)}$ is

$$\tau_k^{(j)*} = \gamma_k^{(j)*} = 1 - \frac{\tau^{\mathrm{UL}}p_k^{(j)*}}{\eta_k^{(j)} \cdot \sum_{i=1}^{N}\left|\sqrt{q^{(i)}}\left(\mathbf{g}_k^{(i,j)}\right)^H \mathbf{w}^{(i)*}\right|^2} \qquad (34)$$

## 4   Simulation Experiment Results and Analysis

In experiment, it is supposed that the total number of cells $N = 7$, cell radius $D = 5$ m, the number of users in each cell $K = 2$, the base station is located in the center of cell, the distance between user-$k$ in cell-$i$ and base station in cell-$j$ is $d_k^{(i,j)}$. The geometric distribution of cell is shown in Fig. 2. Taking the center position of the cell where the user is located as the pole, it is assumed that the polar coordinate $\left(d_k^{(j,j)}, \alpha_k^{(j)}\right)$ from the user to the center position satisfies the uniform distribution: $d_k^{(j,j)} \sim \mathcal{U}(0, D)$, $\alpha_k^{(j)} \sim \mathcal{U}(0, 2\pi)$.

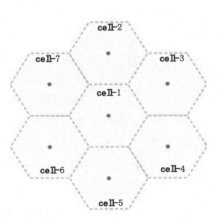

**Fig. 2.** Distribution diagram of total number of cells (N = 7)

Suppose that the number of antennas of each cell base station in each cell is $M = 3$, the downlink transmission power of the base station in each cell is $q^{(j)} = -100$ dBm, the energy capture efficiency of each user: $\eta_k^{(j)} = 0.3$, the maximum uplink transmission power of the user is $p_k^{\max(j)} = -120$ dBm $C = 1$, and the signal-to-noise ratio (SNR) of the user is 20 dB, the channel fading model is $b_k^{(i,j)} = \left(10 \cdot d_k^{(i,j)}\right)^{-1.5}$ and the channel coefficient satisfies $g_{mk}^{(i,j)} \sim \mathcal{CN}\left(0, \left(10 \cdot d_k^{(i,j)}\right)^{-1.5}\right)$. In experiment, we use Monte Carlo method to simulate the distribution probability of channel coefficient.

Assume that the downlink unit time $T = 1$, and it can be divided into 10 time slots. According to the reference [20], the uplink time $\tau^{\text{UL}} = 0.1$, and there are 9 values in the downlink time allocation vector $t^{(j)}$, that is

$$t^{(j)} \in \mathbf{T}^{K \times 1} = \left\{[0.1 \ 0.9]^T \ [0.2 \ 0.8]^T \ [0.3 \ 0.7]^T \dots [0.9 \ 0.1]^T\right\} \qquad (35)$$

We analyzed three groups of comparative simulation experiments, that is, the base station in the uplink was detected by ZF, MRC and MMSE algorithms respectively. In the experiment, the scheme proposed in this paper and the traditional scheme adopted the following transmission methods:

(1) Traditional transmission scheme. In the uplink phase, each user transmits information with the maximum transmit power (i.e. $\mathbf{p}^{(j)} = \mathbf{p}^{max(j)}$). In the downlink stage, each base station transmits information with the average distribution time of each user (i.e. $\mathbf{t}^{(j)} = [0.5 \ 0.5]^T$).

(2) The transmission scheme proposed in this paper. In the uplink stage, each user transmits information with the optimal power based on uplink base station detection method (i.e. $\mathbf{p}^{(j)} = \mathbf{p}_{ZF}^{(j)*}, \mathbf{p}_{MRC}^{(j)*}$, or $\mathbf{p}_{MMSE}^{(j)*}$). In the downlink stage, each base station transmits information with the optimal time allocation(i.e. $\mathbf{t}^{(j)} = \mathbf{t}^{(j)*}$).

Compared with the minimum transmission rate, the simulation results are shown in Figs. 3, 4 and 5.

Based on the above three simulation results, the ratio of the minimum transmission rate of the proposed scheme and the traditional scheme is shown in Table 1. For ZF detection, since its optimal power distribution is $\mathbf{p}_{ZF}^{(j)*} = \mathbf{p}^{max(j)}$, the uplink transmission mode of two schemes is actually the same. From the simulation results, each data in Fig. 3 is identical in the direction of the horizontal axis (minimum uplink transmission rate). For MMSE detection, formulas (9) and (11) show that MMSE is similar to ZF, so that the uplink optimal power allocation can only increase the uplink transmission rate by less than 10%. For the downlink stage, the optimal time allocation method can increase the minimum transmission rate by more than 60%.

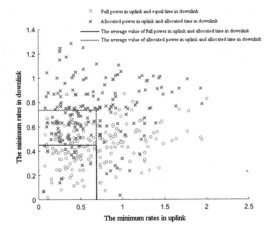

**Fig. 3.** The minimum uplink and downlink transmission rate for each user with UL ZF detection

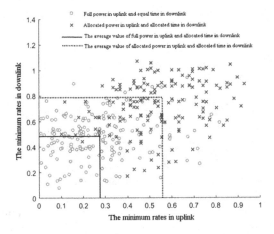

**Fig. 4.** The minimum uplink and downlink transmission rate for each user with UL MRC detection.

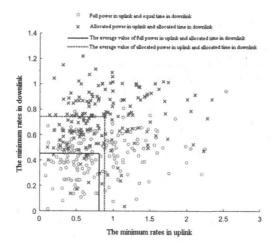

**Fig. 5.** The minimum uplink and downlink transmission rate for each user with UL MMSE detection

**Table 1.** The ratio of the minimum rates of the proposed scheme and traditional scheme.

| Detector in uplink | The ratio of the rates of uplink | The ratio of the rates of downlink |
|---|---|---|
| ZF detector in | 100.00% | 164.14% |
| MRC detector | 201.76% | 162.44% |
| MMSE detector | 109.17% | 163.93% |

## 5  Conclusions

Based on the capture-transmission protocol on the WPCN, a new scheme of joint transmission of energy and information in cellular cell is proposed in this paper, which applies the SWIPT to the downlink transmission of WPCN, and realizes downlink energy transmission and two-way information transmission between base station and users. The scheme describes and optimizes the problem by nonlinear programming, and the whole problem is sequentially divided into upper and lower parts. In the uplink stage, the uplink transmission power of each user in each cell is solved by optimizing the specific objective function, and the solved result is input to the downlink stage as a parameter. In the downlink stage, the specific objective function is optimized to solve the beamforming vector for the base station in each cell and the time allocation vector for energy capture and information decoding for each user group. Simulation results show that compared with the traditional transmission method, this scheme can significantly improve the minimum transmission rate of users.

**Acknowledgments.** These works are supported by the NNSF of China (No. 61762010).

# References

1. Ulukus, S., Yener, A., Erkip, E., et al.: Energy harvesting wireless communications: a review of recent advances. IEEE J. Sel. Areas Commun. **33**(3), 360–381 (2015)
2. Zhang, R., Ho, C.K.: MIMO broadcasting for simultaneous wireless information and power transfer. IEEE Trans. Wirel. Commun. **12**(5), 1989–2001 (2013)
3. Zhou, X., Zhang, R., Ho, C.K.: Wireless information and power transfer: architecture design and rate-energy tradeoff. IEEE Trans. Commun. **61**(11), 4754–4767 (2013)
4. Lu, Y., Xiong, K., Fan, P.: Robust transmit beamforming with artificial redundant signals for secure SWIPT systems under non-linear EH model. IEEE Trans. Wirel. Commun. **17**(4), 2218–2232 (2018)
5. Zeng, Y., Zhang, R.: Optimized training design for wireless energy transfer. IEEE Trans. Commun. **63**(2), 536–550 (2015)
6. Liu, L., Zhang, R., Chua, K.C.: Multi-antenna wireless powered communication with energy beamforming. IEEE Trans. Commun. **62**(12), 4349–4361 (2014)
7. Lu, Y., Xiong, K., Fan, P.: Coordinated beamforming with artificial noise for secure SWIP tunder non-linear EH model: centralized and distributed designs. IEEE J. Sel. Areas Commun. **36**(7), 1544–1563 (2018)
8. Ju, H., Zhang, R.: Throughput maximization in wireless powered communication networks. IEEE Trans. Wirel. Commun. **14**(1), 418–428 (2014)
9. Wang, W., Li, L., Sun, Q., et al.: Power allocation in multiuser MIMO systems for simultaneous wireless information and power transfer. In: 2013 IEEE 78th Vehicular Technology Conference, pp. 1–5. IEEE, Las Vegas (2013)
10. Ju, H., Zhang, R.: Optimal resource allocation in full-duplex wireless-powered communication network. IEEE Trans. Commun. **62**(10), 3528–3540 (2014)
11. Alemayehu, T.S., Kim, J.H., Yoon, W.: Full-duplex distributed massive MIMO system with optimal beamforming and resource allocation for WPCN. J. Commun. Technol. Electron. **62**(12), 1383–1387 (2017)
12. Huang, C., Zhang, R., Cui, S.: Throughput maximization for the gaussian relay channel with energy harvesting constraints. IEEE J. Sel. Areas Commun. **31**(8), 1469–1479 (2013)
13. Gurakan, B., Ozel, O., Yang, J., et al.: Energy cooperation in energy harvesting communications. IEEE Trans. Commun. **61**(12), 4884–4898 (2013)
14. Nasir, A.A., Zhou, X., Durrani, S., et al.: Relaying protocols for wireless energy harvesting and information processing. IEEE Trans. Wirel. Commun. **12**(7), 3622–3636 (2013)
15. Ju, H., Zhang, R.: User cooperation in wireless powered communication networks. In: 2014 IEEE Global Communications Conference, pp. 1430–1435. IEEE, Austin (2014)
16. Bi, S., Zhang, R.: Placement optimization of energy and information access points in wireless powered communication networks. IEEE Trans. Wirel. Commun. **15**(3), 2351–2364 (2016)
17. Chen, H., Xiao, L., Yang, D., et al.: User cooperation in wireless powered communication networks with a pricing mechanism. IEEE Access **5**, 16895–16903 (2017)
18. Kim, N., Lee, Y., Park, H.: Performance analysis of MIMO system with linear MMSE receiver. IEEE Trans. Wirel. Commun. **7**(11), 4474–4478 (2008)
19. Luo, Z.Q., Ma, W.K., So, M.C., et al.: Semidefinite relaxation of quadratic optimization problems. IEEE Sig. Process. Mag. **27**(3), 20–34 (2010)
20. Hiroshi, N.: Prototype implementation of ambient RF energy harvesting wireless sensor networks. Int. J. Eng. Technol. **5**(2), 1282–1287 (2013)

# Short Text Similarity Hybrid Algorithm for a Chinese Medical Intelligent Question Answering System

Huaizhong Liang[1,2], Kaibiao Lin[1,2], and Shunzhi Zhu[1,2(✉)]

[1] School of Computer and Information Engineering,
Xiamen University of Technology, Xiamen 361024, China
zhusz99@qq.com
[2] Engineering Research Center for Medical Data Mining and Application
of Fujian Province, Xiamen 361024, China

**Abstract.** The medical-oriented intelligent question answering (QA) system, which provides users with fast and accurate answers, has gradually caught the attention of the medical and health research community. In a QA system, one of the critical processes is determining how to calculate the textual similarity and match it, for example, the similarity between the question asked by a user and the question as it exists in the system template. However, the question texts are shorter, individual noisy words pose new challenges for semantic parsing of the entire text. In this paper, we propose a new shared layer-based convolutional neural network (SH-CNN) model to calculate the semantic similarity of Chinese short text. The SH-CNN uses a shared layer to extract the prominent features from a pair of questions and then yields textual similarity based on their features. Concurrently, our approach employs the term frequency-inverse document frequency (TF-IDF) algorithm in the feature extraction process, reducing the interference of noisy words during short text similarity calculations. The experimental results show that the textual similarity hybrid algorithm combining SH-CNN and TF-IDF achieves a successful performance in our intelligent QA system and demonstrates a meaningful application value.

**Keywords:** Intelligent question answering system · Convolutional neural network · Short text similarity

## 1 Introduction

A question answering (QA) system is an advanced form of information retrieval [1]; it can answer users' questions with accurate and concise natural language. The medical field is an important direction for information development, and combining it with intelligent QA can accelerate information construction in the medical field. Moreover, with the rapid development of artificial intelligence and

© Springer Nature Singapore Pte Ltd. 2020
W. Hong et al. (Eds.): NCCSTE 2019, CCIS 1216, pp. 129–142, 2020.
https://doi.org/10.1007/978-981-15-5390-5_11

natural language processing technology, some intelligent QA systems for application in the medical field have been designed and proposed, such as LiveMedQA [2], MedTruth [3] and the novel KB method QA [4] for answering medical questions in TREC-CDS. However, research on intelligent QA systems for the medical field is still in its initial development stage, particularly in the Chinese domain. In the Chinese QA community, the greatest challenge is how to understand the Chinese natural language questions asked by users. To solve this problem, we use the template matching method. In this paper, we design a general question template for each type of question asked by users. On this basis, we can understand the user question by calculating the semantic similarity between the user question and the question template, which determines the users' intention and offers them the corresponding answer.

Short text semantic similarity calculations have long been considered a troublesome issue in natural language processing. Individual noisy words will interfere with the entire text due to its short text length. For example, the question "What are the symptoms of a cold?" is similar to the textual expression of another question "What are the complications of a cold?". However, they represent different types of questions. The first one is asking the symptoms of the disease, while the other is querying the complications of the disease.

Some works proposed methods to solve the noise interference in short text similarity calculations with the depth of sentence analysis [5]. First, a word-based method is proposed, which only considers the frequency and part-of-speech information of the words that constitute the sentence [6,7]. The word-based methods only consider the surface information of the sentence and ignore the similarity of the overall structure of the sentence, which leads to certain limitations in the calculation of textual similarity. The second one is a semantic-based method, which analyzes the semantics of words expressed in sentences to find semantic dependencies and calculates similarity on this basis [8,9]. However, these methods are greatly affected by the dependency analysis. In some specific fields, it is difficult to guarantee the accuracy of the dependency analysis results.

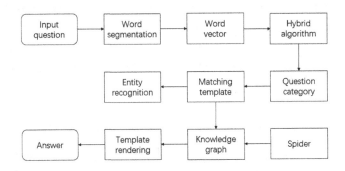

**Fig. 1.** Question and answer system flowchart.

The text similarity calculation is a complicated process, especially in the Chinese environment. Thus, a method that can comprehensively consider multilevel information is needed to compensate for the shortcomings of existing methods. Therefore, we propose a textual similarity hybrid algorithm combining a shared layer-based convolutional neural network (SH-CNN) and term frequency-inverse document frequency (TF-IDF) to extract features from multiple perspectives and grasp the meaning of the text. The procedure of the textual similarity hybrid algorithm in the entire QA system is shown in Fig. 1.

The experimental results show that our method has achieved good results in the task of short text similarity calculations, and our medical-oriented QA system based on this method also shows a successful performance.

## 2 Related Work

In recent years, deep learning has achieved remarkable results in natural language processing tasks, and many deep learning models have been proposed to handle short text similarity.

Regarding models based on the CNN, Yin et al. [10] proposed an attention-based convolutional neural network (ABCNN). The combination of the attention mechanism and CNN was applied to the modeling of sentences. Its essence is to employ the attention mechanism to treat the original independent sentences, consider the correlation between the sentences, and construct a new sentence model containing the context relationship of the sentences. Kalchbrenner et al. [11] proposed a dynamic convolutional neural network (DCNN) for the semantic modeling of sentences. The DCNN uses dynamic K-max pooling to extract the k highest eigenvalues of the text. Surprisingly, the DCNN does not require any prior knowledge, such as syntactic dependency trees, and considers the semantic information between words that are far apart in the sentence. Yao et al. [12] designed a new method of word embedding to construct a three-dimensional feature tensor of the sentence. The authors combined it with a CNN to generate a sentence vector. Finally, the sentence vector pair was calculated to obtain the similarity.

Among other depth models, Lu and Li et al. [13] constructed a deep neural network model called DeepMatch to match short texts. The innovation lies in the topic model to reflect the co-occurrence relationship of words. Tai et al. [14] proposed a tree-structured long-short-term memory network (Tree-LSTM) to predict the semantic relevance of two sentences. Socher et al. [15] introduced a recursive autoencoder (RAE), which measures the similarity between two sentences by learning the feature vectors of phrases in the grammar tree. Different from the work mentioned above, this paper combines deep learning models with traditional TF-IDF algorithms, extracts the in-depth features of text through SH-CNN, and utilized the processed TF-IDF to identify specific words that are prone to noise in medical questions. To accelerate the model training, we adopt a shallow CNN and make some modifications to the network. The experimental results show that the shallow network has also achieved a better result.

## 3    Short Text Similarity Hybrid Algorithm

The QA system designed in this paper can answer seventeen types of questions. Therefore, what we need to accomplish is a classification task, that is, a means to determine which question type the question proposed by the user belongs to. However, the problem is that we need to design numerous corpora for each type of question to train the network, which undoubtedly adds a considerable workload to our task. Therefore, we transform the classification task into a short text similarity calculation task. By designing a general question template for each type of question and processing the textual similarity between the user-proposed question and all question templates, we can obtain the proper question type. In this section, we will describe the proposed short text similarity hybrid algorithm. The entire algorithm consists of two parts: (1) The SH-CNN model: By designing a shared layer to map and process two different questions, the input of the model is the question itself, which is a sequence of words. Because the input questions are symmetric, the model for the first problem can be reused for the second problem. (2) The TF-IDF algorithm: According to the particularity of medical questions, the processed TF-IDF is used to distinguish certain words that may produce noise. The flowchart of the hybrid algorithm is shown below (Fig. 2).

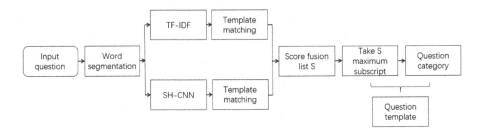

**Fig. 2.** Textual similarity hybrid algorithm

### 3.1    SH-CNN Model

The CNN is often used for various classification tasks [16–18]. The feature information of text or pictures is extracted through convolutional and pooling layers. Then, the feature information is combined nonlinearly by the fully connected layer to obtain the output. To date, the CNN has achieved excellent results in extracting textual features. However, for short texts, due to the short text length, textual features have an essential impact on text distinction. Therefore, it is feasible to extract the salient features of the text through a CNN and then perform similarity calculations. The overall architecture of SH-CNN in this paper is shown in Fig. 3, which is mainly divided into two parts.

**Part a. Text Preprocessing:** This part divides and converts the original text into a sequence of words, then converts each word in the word sequence into a word number (each word has a unique number), and finally expands each element in the word's number sequence into a vector form.

**Part b. Shared Layer:** Different from the input layer of the ordinary CNN, the model designed in this paper contains an extra input so that our input layer can be used to accept a pair of questions. Subsequently, the layer expands the two texts into a sequence of word vectors, and then, the similarity is calculated through the network layer.

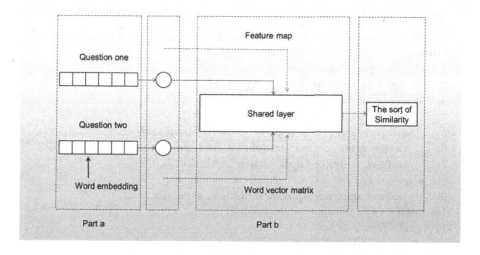

**Fig. 3.** SH-CNN architecture diagram

**Text Preprocessing.** Generally, the CNN is used to process two-dimensional matrices similar to images. For example, a picture can be represented as a two-dimensional array composed of pixel width × pixel height. To apply a CNN to text, we need to convert the training text composed of natural language into a dense vector that the computer can understand. Word2vec [19, 20] is a group of models used to generate word vectors. The so-called word vector is used in a neural network that trains each word as an n-dimensional vector, where the value of each dimension represents part of the feature of the word. In the word2vec model, the spatial distance of words with similar semantics in the word vector representation method is close, such as vector ("Madrid")-vector ("Spain") + vector ("France") is closer to vector ("Paris") more than any other word vector. Before using word2vec, certain preprocessing of the data is required. The training data set used in this paper includes specific Chinese questions, such as "What are the symptoms of a cold?", "Complications of gout" and so on. We use the Chinese word segmentation tool Jieba to segment the text, then build a dictionary $V$ of the words that appear, and encode a unique index number for each word. For example, the dictionary established for the above data set is cold:

0, are: 1, symptoms: 2, of: 3, what: 4, gout: 5, Complications: 6. In this way, the first text in the training set can be expressed as 0, 1, 2, 3, 4, and then, we pad the word index to add each sentence to a fixed length m. The significance of padding is that it allows data to be processed in batches because each example in the batch must have the same length. Through the data preprocessing operation, we can convert Chinese questions into an $n \times m$ array that the CNN can process, where m represents the number of words in each text sequence, and $n$ represents the dimension of the word vector. The padding operation pseudo code is shown below.

---

**Algorithm 1.** Padding operation

**Input:** The input sentences, padding_word=$\langle PAD/ \rangle$ , sequence_length=50
**Output:** The padded_ sentences;

---

1: $function \quad padding$
2: $for \quad i = 0 \quad to \quad len(sentences) \quad do$
3: $\quad sentence = sentence[i]$
4: $\quad if \quad sequence_length > len(sentence) \quad then$
5: $\quad \quad num\_padding \quad = \quad sequence\_length - len(sentence)$
6: $\quad \quad new\_sentence \quad = \quad sentence + num\_padding * [padding\_word]$
7: $\quad \quad padded\_sentences.append(new\_sentence)$
8: $\quad else$
9: $\quad \quad padded\_sentence.append(sentence[: sequence\_length])$
10: $\quad end \quad if$
11: $\quad end \quad for$
12: $return \quad padded\_sentence$
13:$end \quad function$

---

**Shared Layer.** As shown in Fig. 4, the entire shared layer consists of a convolutional layer, a pooling layer, and a fully connected layer, which is used to process the two text word vector matrices that are input in the horizontal direction. Finally, the captured feature information is stitched together through the fully connected layer, and then, the similarity of the sentence vectors is calculated.

To clearly describe the convolutional calculation process, we first represent a text sequence $S = (x_1, x_2, ..., x_m)$ consisting of m words as a word vector matrix:

$$S_w = (x_1^T, x_2^T, ..., x_m^T) \tag{1}$$

Each word in S comes from the dictionary $V$, and $x_i^T \in R^n$ represents the n-dimensional word vector of the i-th word in the text sequence $S$, $S_w \in R^{n \times m}$, as shown in the word matrix in Fig. 4. The convolutional filter runs on $S_w$ and extracts the features. The convolution formula is:

$$C = Relu(\phi \cdot x_{i-j}^T + b) \tag{2}$$

When processing a text sequence, the convolution filter $\phi$ can only move in the "up and down" direction of the word vector matrix $S_w$, and its size is $|\phi| =$

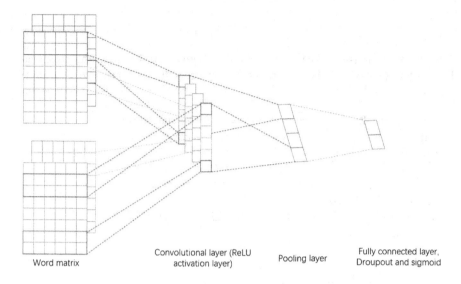

Word matrix | Convolutional layer (ReLU activation layer) | Pooling layer | Fully connected layer, Droupout and sigmoid

**Fig. 4.** Structure of the shared layer model

$j - i + 1$. As in formula (2), take the dot product of $\phi$ and $x_{i-j}^T$ ($x_{i-j}^T$ refers to the concatenation of the vector group $x_i^T, x_{i+1}^T, ..., x_j^T$) to obtain a new one-dimensional feature vector $C^* = \{C_1, C_2, ..., C_{m-j+i}\}$, where $C_i$ represents the local eigenvalue generated during each step of the convolution filter. The essence of convolution filter $\phi$ is an n-gram feature extractor. The features extracted by different sizes of convolution filters are different. For text classification tasks, the convolution filter size is usually set to 5; while for short texts, this size is too large and will introduce noise, making it difficult for the CNN to extract the textual features we expect. However, if the size of the convolutional filter is too small, a complete word representation cannot be extracted. Therefore, we take multiple convolution filters of different sizes to test and combine them arbitrarily; the final selected convolution filter size is 3. During the neural network training process, $k$ different types of convolution filters are initialized, and each convolution filter extracts a feature vector. As shown in the convolutional layer in Fig. 4, $k$ one-dimensional feature vectors are finally obtained. To extract the most prominent features of the text, we choose the maximum pooling operation and take the maximum value of the $k$ one-dimensional vectors obtained after the convolution. Then, they are stitched together to finally obtain a vector with a structure of $k1$ dimensions as the output of this layer. A dropout is performed after the pooling layer, which is activated with a probability $p$, and the neuron connection is modified by randomly deleting the neurons. In simple terms, when the forward propagation is performed, the activation value of a certain neuron will stop working with probability $p$. This method can make our model more generalizable. Finally, according to the needs of the task, a sigmoid is selected as the activation layer. The layer accepts a vector representation of the two texts after the dropout.

$$S(x) = \frac{1}{1 + e^{-x}} \tag{3}$$

The output value is a floating-point number between 0–1. This value represents the similarity between the two texts. The larger the value is, the greater the similarity.

---

**Algorithm 2.** The calculation process of the shared layer

---

**Input:** The input Word vector $matrix, matrix_1, matrix_2$;
**Output:** Similarity score;

---

1: *Initialize   the   filter* : $filter^1, filter^2, ..., filter^k$
2: $merged\_input = Concatenate([matrix_1, matrix_2])$
3: *for* $i = 1$ *to* $k - 1$ *do*
4:   $conv = ReLU(convolute(merged\_input, filter^i))$
5:     $merged\_vector = Maxpooling(conv)$
6: *end   for*
7: $dense = Dense(k, ReLU)(merged\_vector)$
8: $dropout = Dropout(dense)$
9: *Similarity   score* $= Dense(1, sigmoid)(dropout)$

---

## 3.2   TF-IDF

TF-IDF is a commonly used weighting technique for information query and information exploration. TF-IDF is used in this paper to evaluate the importance of a word to a sentence in the corpus. TF is the word frequency, which refers to the frequency of a word in a given file. Its importance can be expressed as:

$$\text{tf}_{i,j} = \frac{n_{i,j}}{\sum_k n_{k,j}} \tag{4}$$

Among the variables, the numerator is the number of occurrences of the word in the file, and the denominator is the sum of the occurrences of all the words in the file. IDF is the inverse document frequency. First, the total number of documents is divided by the number of documents containing the word, and the logarithm of the obtained quotient is taken, that is:

$$\text{idf}_i = log\frac{|D|}{|\{j : t_i \in d_j\}|} \tag{5}$$

And Then

$$\text{tfidf}_{i,j} = \text{tf}_{i,f} \times idf_i \tag{6}$$

High-frequency words in a particular file, as well as low file frequencies of the words in the entire file set, can generate a high-weight TF-IDF. Therefore, when a word has a high TF in one file and rarely appears in other files, the word is considered to have a good discrimination ability. The performance of TF-IDF is of great significance in helping us identify certain noisy words. The reason is that in this paper, we set up a file for each question template, and the file contains some essential words appearing in the template and words similar to it. For example, for the question template "What are the symptoms of a cold?", the file contains words such as symptoms, phenomena, manifestations, and some short sentences containing these words. Since each template represents a different type of question, these words do not appear in the files corresponding to other question templates. Concurrently, for some words that are not helpful in determining the type of question, such as "cold", "of", and "what", we delete them to eliminate the interference caused by these words. Therefore, for the text "What are the symptoms of a cold?" and "What are the complications of a cold?", "symptoms" and "complications" are specially weighted in the set file, and even though the two texts are similar, TF-IDF can also distinguish between them. We combine the textual similarity score obtained by the SH-CNN model with the score obtained by TF-IDF to determine the question template corresponding to the question submitted by the user.

## 4    Experimental Results and Analysis

In this section, we introduce the dataset, word2vec model, parameter settings, and loss function used in the training process.

### 4.1    Training

Our experimental data set is LCQMC (a large-scale Chinese question matching corpus) [21]. LCQMC is a question semantic matching data set constructed by Harbin Institute of Technology at the Natural Language Processing International Summit COLING2018. Its goal is to judge the semantic similarity of two questions. The data set first selects high-frequency questions in different fields, such as Baidu QA education and medical treatment. After the preliminary screening through the Wasserstein distance, the data set is finally labeled manually. On this basis, this paper adds thousands of medical question pairs for the questions involved in the system. The correlation scores for all question pairs are marked as 0 or 1.

The word2vec model used in this paper is trained from the 268G Chinese corpus, including more than 8 million Baidu Encyclopedia news articles and 4 million Sohu news articles. The Chinese word segmentation tool of the training corpus is Jieba, and all non-Chinese characters are excluded. The size of the model after training is 3.1 GB, and the word dimension is 128 dimensions.

The hyper parameters of the model were set as follows: After repeated tests, the size of the convolutional filter was set to 3, 128 different convolutional filters were used for feature extraction, the size of a batch was 64, and the dropout rate was set to 0.5.

Our training model uses a cross-entropy loss function:

$$loss = -\frac{1}{n} \sum_{i=1}^{n} [\hat{y}_i \log y_i + (1 - \hat{y}_i) \log(1 - \hat{y}_i)] \tag{7}$$

where $y_i$ represents that the sample $i$ belongs to $y$, $\hat{y}_i$ represents the probability of its establishment, and $n$ is the size of the training set. *Loss* is 0 only when $y_i$ and $\hat{y}_i$ are equal; otherwise *loss* is a positive number, and the value of *loss* will increase as the probability difference increases.

## 4.2    Experiment Analysis

At present, there is no relevant question pair corpus of Chinese medical questions. For the question template designed in this system, we crawl various types of real questions from medical and health websites for matching and verification. To demonstrate the performance of the hybrid algorithm, we use TF-IDF [6], the Jaccard [7] coefficient, word2vec [22], cosine similarity [23] and SH-CNN to calculate textual similarity, and compare these results with the results of the hybrid algorithm.

For the evaluation of the QA system performance, we must consider not only the accuracy of the QA system but also the runtime. Because the QA system itself is designed to provide convenience for the user, if the system runs too long, even if it has a high precision, the implementation is meaningless. As shown in Table 1, SH-CNN has achieved excellent results in the processing of textual similarity, and the program does not take a long time. Compared with the traditional textual similarity algorithm, SH-CNN builds a network model by learning from a plethora of texts and uses this model to integrate and calculate the prominent features from the texts, thereby obtaining the deep semantic information of the texts. The traditional textual similarity algorithm pays more attention to some surface information such as word frequency in the text or similarities and differences between the limited sample sets so that it provides a lower accuracy.

**Table 1.** Results of five different methods tables.

|  |  | Running time | Accuracy |
|---|---|---|---|
| • | TF-IDF | 0.893 s | 77.91% |
| • | Jaccard | 0.034 s | 68.60% |
| • | SH-CNN | 0.812 s | **82.56%** |
| • | Word2vec | 63.425 s | 60.47% |
| • | Cosine | **0.003 s** | 58.14% |

Natural Chinese language is complicated and possesses a variety of expressions. The semantic information of the text should be understood from multiple perspectives. Since word2vec takes too long to process textual similarity and the accuracy is not satisfactory, we eliminate this method and combine the remaining four methods to verify further.

**Table 2.** Nodes corresponding to the hybrid algorithm.

| A | SH-CNN+TF-IDF |
|---|---|
| B | Cosine+SH-CNN |
| C | Jaccard+SH-CNN |
| D | Jaccard+Cosine |
| E | Jaccard+TF-IDF |
| F | Jaccard+TF-IDF |

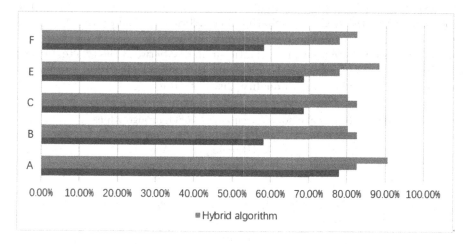

**Fig. 5.** Test results of the hybrid algorithm

Figure 5 shows the original accuracy of each algorithm, and the accuracy obtained after mixing each of the two algorithms. Table 2 presents the nodes corresponding to each hybrid algorithm. We know from Fig. 5 that algorithm combinations affect the original results, whereas some algorithm combinations can significantly improve the accuracy of the algorithm. With the combination of appropriate algorithms, an understanding of semantic information in Chinese text from different perspectives can be obtained without reduced accuracy.

According to Table 3, the hybrid algorithm combining SH-CNN and TF-IDF achieves the best results. After adding TF-IDF to SH-CNN, the average response time of the system increased from 0.812 s to 2.342 s. These different algorithms and hybrid algorithms compute and match textual information based on various aspects. Specifically, in these traditional textual similarity calculation methods, the TF-IDF algorithm has the highest accuracy; it is used to evaluate the importance of a word for a file set or a file in a corpus. In the case of setting the appropriate corpus, the TF-IDF can achieve excellent results for the short text relevant to this paper. However, the traditional text similarity algorithm only focuses on the similarity of the text itself, and inevitably has some shortcomings. In addition, when the feature words in some sentences do not appear in the corpus, and no special weight is applied, the processing result of TF-IDF is hardly satisfactory. Therefore, we need the CNN and word vectors. The word vector is required because of its inherent properties which we mentioned in the text processing section. Concurrently, we need the CNN to extract the prominent features in the sentence and combine them for analysis. The CNN only needs the filter to find these features, and does so regardless of where they appear. Hence, combining the SH-CNN with TF-IDF to process textual similarity yields the best results. Compared with the hybrid algorithm of SH-CNN and TF-IDF, the combination of traditional textual similarity calculation methods lacks the preprocessing of Chinese text content and generates interference of noise in the process of calculating textual similarity. The hybrid algorithm understands the textual information from the deep semantic information and the surface textual information to calculate the semantic similarity between the two texts. The experimental results have shown that using this hybrid algorithm can ensure that the system provides a high-quality answer to users.

**Table 3.** Comparison of accuracy of different algorithms.

|               | Running time | Accuracy |
| ------------- | ------------ | -------- |
| SH-CNN        | **0.812 s**  | 82.56%   |
| TF-IDF        | 0.893 s      | 77.91%   |
| SH-CNN+TF-IDF | 2.342 s      | **90.70%** |
| SH-CNN        | 0.812 s      | **82.56%** |
| Cosine        | **0.003 s**  | 58.14%   |
| Cosine+SH-CNN | 2.254 s      | 80.23%   |
| SH-CNN        | 0.812 s      | **82.56%** |
| Jaccard       | **0.034 s**  | 68.60%   |
| Jaccard+SH-CNN | 2.281 s     | 80.23%   |
| Cosine        | **0.003 s**  | 58.14%   |
| Jaccard       | 0.034 s      | **68.60%** |
| Jaccard+Cosine | 0.019 s     | 61.62%   |
| TF-IDF        | 0.893 s      | 77.91%   |
| Jaccard       | **0.034 s**  | 68.60%   |
| Jaccard+TF-IDF | 0.096 s     | **88.37%** |
| TF-IDF        | 0.893 s      | 77.91%   |
| Cosine        | **0.003 s**  | 58.14%   |
| Cosine+TF-IDF | 0.093 s      | **82.54%** |

## 5   Conclusion

This paper proposes a hybrid algorithm combining the SH-CNN and TF-IDF algorithms to calculate Chinese textual similarity, thus, completing the design and implementation of a Chinese medical intelligent QA system. Compared to the CNN model commonly used for text categorization, we use the CNN to calculate textual similarity, where the input of the model is a pair of questions. The shared layer is used to deal with the two questions separately, and finally, the similarity score among the pairs of questions is obtained. Considering the diversity and complexity of Chinese text semantics, we use this hybrid algorithm to grasp textual information from multiple perspectives, and the experimental results also prove the system's effectiveness. In further work, we consider adding an attention mechanism to SH-CNN to obtain more detailed information from the text and to suppress useless information interference. Concurrently, we also focus on the optimization of the word2vec model to explore the similarity between the deep semantics of Chinese texts.

**Acknowledgments.** This work is supported by the joint Funds of Scientific and Technological Innovation Program of Fujian Province (No. 2017Y9059), the Joint Funds of 5th Round of Health and Education Research Program of Fujian Province (No. 2019-WJ-41), the Science Foundation of the Fujian Province (No. 2018J01577), the Xiamen Science and Technology Planning Project (No. 3502Z20179028), and the Science and Technology Planning Project of XMUT (No. YKJCX2019040, YKJ16019R).

# References

1. Zhou, G., Huang, J.: Modeling and learning continuous word embedding with metadata for question retrieval. IEEE Trans. Knowl. Data Eng. 1
2. Yang, Y., Yu, J., Hu, Y., et al.: CMU LiveMedQA at TREC 2017 LiveQA: a consumer health question answering system
3. Deng, Y., Li, Y., Shen, Y., et al.: MedTruth: a semi-supervised approach to discovering knowledge condition information from multi-source medical data
4. Goodwin, T.R., Harabagiu, S.M.: Medical question answering for clinical decision support. In: The 25th ACM International (2016)
5. Zhou, F.G.: New method for sentence similarity computing and its application in question answering system. Comput. Eng. Appl. **44**(1), 165–168 (2008)
6. Joachims, T.: A probabilistic analysis of the Rocchio algorithm with TFIDF for text categorization. In: International Conference on Machine Learning (1996)
7. Zhang, X.L., Ying-Zi, F.U., Chu, P.X., et al.: Application of Jaccard Similarity coefficient in recommender system. Comput. Technol. Dev. **24**, 158–165 (2015)
8. Nivre, J.: Deterministic dependency parsing of English text (2004)
9. Che, W., Li, Z., Liu, T.: LTP: a Chinese language technology platform. In: COLING 2010, 23rd International Conference on Computational Linguistics, Demonstrations Volume, 23–27 August 2010, Beijing, China (2010)
10. Yin, W., Schütze, H., Bing, X., et al.: ABCNN: attention-based convolutional neural network for modeling sentence pairs. Comput. Sci. **4**, 259–272 (2015)
11. Kalchbrenner, N., Grefenstette, E., Blunsom, P.: A convolutional neural network for modelling sentences. Eprint Arxiv, 1 (2014)
12. Yao, H., Liu, H., Zhang, P.: A novel sentence similarity model with word embedding based on convolutional neural network: sentence similarity model with word embedding based on convolutional neural network. Concurr. Comput. Pract. Exp. **30**(1), e4415 (2018)

13. Lu, Z., Li, H.: A deep architecture for matching short texts. In: Advances in Neural Information Processing Systems, pp. 1367–1375 (2013)
14. Tai, K.S., Socher, R., Manning, C.D.: Improved semantic representations from tree-structured long short-term memory networks. arXiv preprint arXiv:1503.00075 (2015)
15. Socher, R., Huang, E.H., Pennin, J., et al.: Dynamic pooling and unfolding recursive autoencoders for paraphrase detection. In: Advances in Neural Information Processing Systems, pp. 801–809 (2011)
16. Kim, Y.: Convolutional neural networks for sentence classification. Eprint Arxiv (2014)
17. Zhang, Y., Wallace, B.: A sensitivity analysis of (and practitioners' guide to) convolutional neural networks for sentence classification
18. He, T., Zhang, Z., Zhang, H., et al.: Bag of tricks for image classification with convolutional neural networks
19. Mikolov, T., Sutskever, I., Chen, K., et al.: Distributed representations of words and phrases and their compositionalit. Adv. Neural Inf. Process. Syst. **26**, 3111–3119 (2013)
20. Mikolov, T., Chen, K., Corrado, G., et al.: Efficient estimation of word representations in vector space. arXiv preprint arXiv:1301.3781 (2013)
21. Liu, X., Chen, Q., Deng, C., et al.: LCQMC: a large-scale Chinese question matching corpus. In: Proceedings of the 27th International Conference on Computational Linguistics, pp. 1952–1962 (2018)

# Indoor Positioning Model Based on Optimized Lighting Search Algorithm

Chunzhi Wang[1], Xin Wang[1], Shang Pan[1], Siwei Wei[2],
and Lingyu Yan[1(✉)]

[1] School of Computer Science, Hubei University of Technology, Wuhan, China
{wangchunzhi,wangxin,panshang,
yanlingyu}@hbut.edu.cn
[2] CCCC Second Highway Consultants Co., Ltd., Wuhan, China
weisiwei@163.com

**Abstract.** Recently, reasonable and efficient indoor positioning solution is an urgent problem to be solved. Different technologies like cellular positioning technology, radio frequency identification (RFID) positioning technology, Bluetooth positioning technology, ultrasonic positioning technology, and Wi-Fi positioning technology have been proposed. In view of the wide use of Wi-Fi, the high penetration rate of Wi-Fi connected to mobile phones, and the need to re-install signal transmitters to detect signal data, this paper applies signal data from several devices to implement indoor positioning. A chaotic optimization method based on lightning search algorithm support vector regression (CLSA-SVR) for indoor location. Compared with other methods such as particle swarm optimization (PSO), genetic algorithm (GA) and ant colony optimization (ACO) models, the LSA based method has higher prediction accuracy, robustness and stability. According to the method, high-accuracy position information can be quickly obtained, which provides a reference for people's position perception in the room.

**Keywords:** Indoor positioning · Lightning search optimization · Support vector regression · Wireless technology

## 1 Introduction

In recent years, with the rapid development of information technology, the internet has affected people's lives. People have greatly benefited from the development of the internet. Its development has brought convenience to people's lives and allowed people to enter the digital age, such as currency digitization [1], file digitization [2], etc. Since ancient times, mankind has always relied on road signs, from ancient compasses and maps to today's road signs, global positioning systems such as China Beidou Satellite [3], all answering the question "how should I get there?" However, the scale of these problems is the characteristics of the country to the country, the city to the city, and the home to the home, all based on outdoor. In fact, people's activities in the indoor environment also need the help of positioning, especially in large venues such as shopping malls, casinos and other places. Indoors, the GPS signal is extremely weak,

© Springer Nature Singapore Pte Ltd. 2020
W. Hong et al. (Eds.): NCCSTE 2019, CCIS 1216, pp. 143–152, 2020.
https://doi.org/10.1007/978-981-15-5390-5_12

which leads to the failure of the traditional positioning system, which leads researchers to explore the indoor positioning scheme.

The popularity and development of mobile intelligent terminals and wireless local area networks make users' demand for information data more and more urgent, and indoor positioning is particularly important, which provides space for location-based services [4], location-based services (LBS). The basic principle of a location service can be summarized as first measuring the physical location of the reference point, and then using the known physical location reference point to estimate the real-time location of the user.

The remainder of this paper is organized as follows. In Sect. 2, we review the related works. Then we present the Support Vector Regression Machine Positioning Model for Chaotic Lightning Search Algorithm in Sect. 3. In Sect. 4, extensive experiments are conducted to demonstrate the effectiveness and efficiency of the proposed algorithm. Finally, we draw a conclusion in Sect. 5.

## 2    Related Works

Considering that support vector regression machines [5] have better generalization performance, they have better predictive ability when training data is limited. This paper will use support vector regression to perform indoor location prediction based on location fingerprint. In the positioning algorithm, the non-sensitive support vector regression (SVR) was generally used to construct a nonlinear mapping relationship between signal strength and physical location. The main process is shown in Fig. 1.

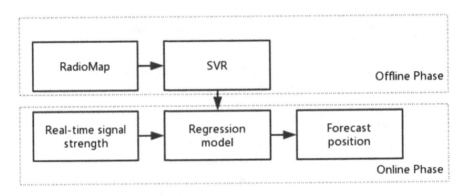

**Fig. 1.** Schematic diagram of indoor wireless positioning based on support vector regression.

In the training process, the error value less than or equal to $\varepsilon$ were regarded as the error being 0, the signal strength sample $(RSS_i, p_i), i = 1\ldots l, RSS_i \in R^d$ obtained on the block $L_i$, the input sample vector is $RSS_i$, the coordinate vector corresponding to the output block $L_i$ is $p_i = (x_i, y_i)$, and the input vector dimension is $d$, this dimension represents the number of WLANs received on the block, constructs a linear regression evaluation function corresponding to $x$ coordinates and $y$ coordinates in a high-dimensional nonlinear space, and achieves the purpose of constructing a nonlinear positioning function according to the evaluation function. Give the regression function of the output position coordinates:

$$x = \langle w, \varphi(RSS) \rangle + b \tag{1}$$

In Eq. (1), $\varphi$ is a nonlinear mapping function that maps the input low-dimensional data to the high-dimensional feature space, $b$ is an offset constant, and $w$ is a weight vector. In order to verify its generalization ability, the following compares the risk function of the learning function $R(w)$:

$$R(w) = \int L(x, f(RSS, w)) dF(RSS, x) \tag{2}$$

$$L(x, f(RSS, w)) = \max(|f(RSS, w) - x| - \epsilon, 0) \tag{3}$$

Let $F(RSS, x)$ be the distribution function of the joint-output joint probability. In general, the $F(RSS, x)$ function was unknown, so the insensitive support vector regression evolves into the following optimization problem according to the principle of minimum risk:

$$\min J(w) = \frac{1}{2} \|w\|^2 + \hat{C} \sum_{i=1}^{l} (\xi_i + \xi_i^*) \tag{4}$$

$$s.t. \begin{cases} (\langle w, \varphi(RSS_i) \rangle + b) - x_i \leq \varepsilon + \xi_i \\ x_i - (\langle w, \varphi(RSS_i) \rangle + b) \leq \varepsilon + \xi_i^* \\ \xi_i^* \geq 0, \xi_i \geq 0, i = 1, 2, \ldots, l \end{cases} \tag{5}$$

In Eqs. (4), first part controls the size of the dimension, which affects the complexity of the regression function. Second part controls the empirical risk of the regression function, which is the training error, $\hat{C}$ is the penalty factor, $w$ can be converted to a number of support vector representations, which can be expressed as:

$$w = \sum_{i=1}^{NSV} \alpha_i \cdot \phi(RSS_i) \tag{6}$$

So the formula (1) can be converted to:

$$x = \sum_{i \in sv} \alpha_i < \phi(RSS_i), \phi(RSS) > + b \tag{7}$$

In Eq. 6, $sv$ is the set of support vectors, and $\alpha_i$ is the corresponding weight coefficient. If use the Gaussian kernel function, $< \phi(RSS_i), \phi(RSS) >$ can obtain this value by calculating the kernel function without displaying the calculation:

$$K(RSS_i, RSS) = \,<\phi(RSS_i), \phi(RSS)> \, = \exp(-\gamma^2||RSS_i - RSS||^2) \qquad (8)$$

In Eq. 7, $K(RSS, RSS_i)$ and $\gamma$ represent the kernel function and the corresponding kernel function parameters respectively. After the conversion, the final Eq. 7 is converted into the support vector regression function as:

$$x = \sum_{i \in sv} \alpha_i K(RSS, RSS_i) + b \qquad (9)$$

The generalization performance of support vector regression method is much higher than that of neural network algorithm. When the training data is limited, it can highlight the excellent generalization performance. After comparison, the method had high generalization ability and fitting ability. In this paper, the lightning search algorithm optimized it, which made the prediction effect of indoor wireless positioning more accurate, and had higher robustness and generalization ability.

Lightning is a fascinating and profound natural phenomenon as shown in Fig. 2. The probabilistic nature and tortuous nature of lightning discharge are due to thunderstorms. Shareef et al. proposed a new heuristic lightning search optimization algorithm (LSA) in 2015 [6], which originated from the natural phenomenon of lightning, through the spatial probability distribution and tortuosity of the discharge body, and the space discharge body. The three discharge bodies of the transitional discharge body and the guided discharge body generate a random distribution function to solve the problem to be optimized. The lightning search algorithm has the advantages of less adjustment parameters, high convergence precision, and strong global search ability. It has been applied to function optimization, travel salesman problem (TSP) optimization and so on.

## 3  Support Vector Regression Machine Positioning Model for Chaotic Lightning Search Algorithm

For the lightning search algorithm, this paper uses the logic self-mapping function to generate the chaotic sequence to initialize the position of the transitional discharge body in the space of the lightning search algorithm. By adding the chaotic process, the search ability of the lightning search algorithm can be improved. The expression function of the self-mapping function is shown in Eq. 10:

$$P_{i+1}^k = 1 - 2(P_i^k)^2, P_i^k \in (-1, 1) \qquad (10)$$

In Eq. 9, the mapping domain is in the $(-1, 0)$ and $(0, 1)$ intervals, and $k$ is the dimension of the search space. If the number of iterations is greater than zero, chaos must occur.

The chaotic lightning search algorithm steps can be summarized as follows:

1. Initialize the lightning search algorithm parameters, set the maximum number of iterations $M$, the number of populations $N$, the time channel $T$ and the initial top energy $E_{sl}$.
2. Use the formula in Eq. (11) logical self-mapping function to generate a chaotic sequence to initialize the spatial position of the group, initialize the position of the transitional discharge body, determine the fitness function (i.e., the function of the target parameter to be optimized), and set the current iteration number $t$.
3. Use the fitness function *fitness* to evaluate the performance of the discharge body, calculate its energy $E_p$.
4. Update the top energy $E_{sl}$ of the space discharge body. If the solution of $E_p < E_{sl}$ or $P^S_{i\_new}$ is better, $P^S_i$ is updated to the position $P^S_{i\_new}$ of the new space discharge body; otherwise it remains unchanged and waits for the next iteration. If $P^S_{i\_new}$ extends to $P^S_{i\_new}$ and it is better than the current iteration, the space discharge body is upgraded to a pilot discharge body.
5. Update the top energy $E_{sl}$ of the pilot discharge body. If $E_p > E_{sl}$, update $P^L$ to the new boot discharge body position $P^L_{new}$; if a better solution is obtained in the $t+1$ iteration, the corresponding rung pilot $sl_i$ is expanded to the new position $sl_{i\_new}$ and $P^L$ is updated to $P^L_{new}$; otherwise, the guide discharge body keep the location of $P^L$ and waiting for the next iteration.
6. Determine whether the channel time reaches $T$. If this value $T$ is reached, the worst channel is eliminated, and the channel time is reset, and the new direction of the discharge body and its new energy $E_p$ are updated; otherwise, the discharge body is directly updated. Its new direction and its new energy is $E_p$.
7. Calculate the discharge body energy $E_p$ according to the fitness function, and expand its channel. If $E_p > E_{sl}$, the discharge body performs cascade pilot propagation or generates a channel, eliminates the channel with lower energy, and updates $P_L$ to $P^{new}_L$; if $E_p \leq E_{sl}$, the position of the leader discharge body $P_L$ remains the same, waiting for the next iteration.
8. Determine if the optimization meets the termination condition, if it is satisfied, to 9, otherwise make t = t + 1 and then go to step 4.
9. At the end of the optimization, the energy discharge of the guided discharge body is performed, and the discharge body of the maximum energy is the optimal solution in the spatial position where it is located.

## 4  Results

This paper quotes Rohra's method, using its seven wireless hotspots in the office, using receivers to receive signal data from different blocks. In the offline phase, it polled every second, and received and received. The signal strength of each wireless hotspot on the device was recorded by the receiver in the block, and the data was sampled in different blocks. The data sample is shown in Table 1 below, and WS1–WS7 respectively indicate receiving. For the signal value of the wireless hotspot, the block indicates the block in which the receiver was located.

**Table 1.** Receiver signal for different wireless hotspots.

| WS1 | WS2 | WS3 | WS4 | WS5 | WS6 | WS7 | Area |
|-----|-----|-----|-----|-----|-----|-----|------|
| −64 | −56 | −61 | −66 | −71 | −82 | −81 | 1 |
| −68 | −57 | −61 | −65 | −71 | −85 | −85 | 1 |
| −17 | −66 | −61 | −37 | −68 | −75 | −77 | 2 |
| −16 | −70 | −58 | −14 | −73 | −71 | −80 | 2 |
| −52 | −48 | −56 | −53 | −62 | −78 | −81 | 3 |
| −49 | −55 | −51 | −49 | −63 | −81 | −73 | 3 |

In order to verify the effect of the CLSA-SVR model, this paper uses the actual data as the simulation data set. The experimental data was from the UCI machine learning database, and the data set name is the wireless indoor localization data set. The data set was derived from actual measurements by Rajen Bhatt et al., and the data collection location is the office environment in which the researcher is located.

The experimental environment of this simulation experiment is as Table 2.

**Table 2.** Model simulation environment.

| Type | Name | Detail |
|------|------|--------|
| Hardware | processor | Intel(R) Core(TM) i5-7400 CPU@3.00 GHz |
| | RAM | 8G |
| Software | System | Microsoft Windows 10 × 64 LTSB |
| | Language | Matlab |
| | Tools | Matlab 2016b;libsvm toolbox; source code |

### 4.1  Data Preprocessing

In order to reduce modeling errors and improve computational efficiency, the data was first standardized. In this paper, the normalization method was used to normalize the data to the 0–1 interval.

$$x_i^* = \frac{x_i - x_{min}}{x_{max} - x_{min}}, i = 1, 2, \cdots, n \tag{11}$$

In the formula in Eq. 10, $x_i, x_i^*$ represents data before and after normalization, $x_{max}$ represents data of the maximum value in the original data, $x_{min}$ represents data of the minimum value in the original data, and $n$ represents the total entry of the data set.

As shown in the left figure in Fig. 2, the data was normalized to the actual location. The Fig. 3 is the practical shuffling method for obfuscating data to make the data randomly normalized. By normalizing and randomizing the data series, the model can achieve faster speeds when performing regression calculations.

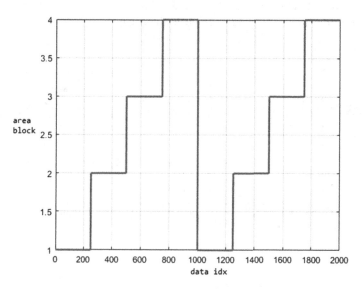

**Fig. 2.** Origin dataset.

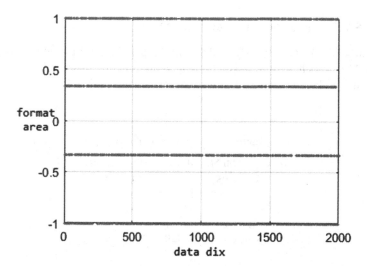

**Fig. 3.** Format dataset

## 4.2    Model Training

In the experiment, the number of iterations was set to 100, and the number of discharge bodies was set to 50. In order to better analyze and predict the position of the infinite user, the first 1600 pieces of data after confusion were used as training data. In this paper, the training data and prediction data were divided into 4:1 to improve the accuracy of the training model. The last 400 data after confusion were used as test data. Finally, the fitting was performed to evaluate the accuracy of the LSA-SVR model.

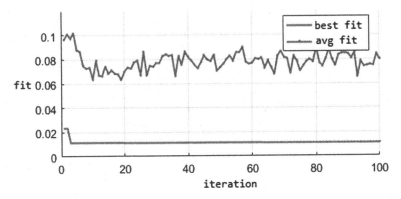

**Fig. 4.** Lightning search optimization algorithm (LSA) fitness line.

Figure 4 shows the fitness of the LSA 100 iterations. Finally, the optimal SVR penalty factor $C = 0.1$ and the optimal Gaussian kernel function parameter $\gamma = 0.14$, $\varepsilon = 0.001$.

## 4.3    CLSA-SVR and Compared to Other Model

In order to verify the CLSA-SVR model of this paper, the SVR model based on PSO, GA, and ACO which were achieved by matlab and run at matlab2016b were used to train and fit the data separately. The results are shown in Table 3.

**Table 3.** Model prediction table.

| Model | MES | MAE | STD of 50 times |
|---|---|---|---|
| GA-SVR | 0.0519 | 0.2129 | 2.3212 |
| ACO-SVR | 0.0621 | 0.2313 | 2.4627 |
| PSO-SVR | 0.0327 | 0.1983 | 2.1331 |
| LSA-SVR | 0.0313 | 0.1231 | 1.6531 |
| CLSA-SVR | 0.0291 | 0.1120 | 1.4919 |

According to the results in Table 3, it can be seen that in the mean square error, the support vector regression machine model MES of the chaotic lightning search algorithm was 0.2918, which had higher prediction accuracy than other models.

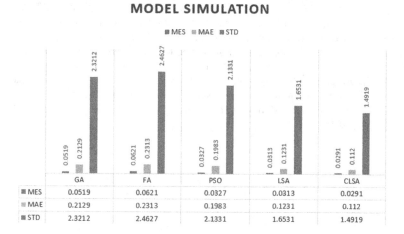

**Fig. 5.** Simulation result columnar comparison chart.

In order to verify the robustness of the model, the above five models are run 50 times, and finally the MES variance is calculated. According to Fig. 5, the variance of the predicted mean square error of the lightning search algorithm model was the smallest, which indicates that the model had better robustness than other models. In summary, the indoor positioning model based on the lightning search algorithm had better prediction effect, and had more efficient, stable and accurate characteristics in indoor positioning, which provides a certain reference value for indoor positioning.

## 5   Conclusions

This paper mainly studies the model of WLAN fingerprint location based on support vector regression machine optimized by lightning search algorithm, and analyzes the robustness, generalization ability and prediction accuracy of the model. It shows that the model has good prediction and localization ability. Robustness has been found to have higher prediction effects. Then the chaotic-based lightning search algorithm is studied and applied to the WLAN fingerprint location model based on support vector regression machine, which further enhances the robustness and prediction performance of the model.

# References

1. Nakamoto, S.: Bitcoin: a peer-to-peer electronic cash system (2008)
2. Parkk, A., Lee, K.J., Casalegno, F.: The three dimensions of book evolution in ubiquitous computing age: digitalization, augmentation, and hypermediation. In: 2010 IEEE International Conference on Sensor Networks, Ubiquitous, and Trustworthy Computing. IEEE (2010)
3. He, S., Chan, S.H.G.: Wi-Fi fingerprint-based indoor positioning: recent advances and comparisons. IEEE Commun. Surv. Tutor. **18**, 466–490 (2016)
4. Yoo, J.W., Park, K.H.: A cooperative clustering protocol for energy saving of mobile devices with wlan and bluetooth interfaces. IEEE Trans. Mob. Comput. **10**, 491–504 (2011)
5. Drucker, H., Burges, C.J.C., Kaufman, L., Smola, A.V.: Support vector regression machines. In: Advances in Neural Information Processing Systems, pp. 155–161 (1997)
6. Shareef, H., Ibrahim, A.A., Mutlag, A.H.: Lightning search algorithm. Appl. Soft Comput. **36**, 315–333 (2015)

# Author Index

Printed in the United States
By Bookmasters